Meteors, Meteorites, and
Meteoroids

Meteors, Meteorites, and Meteoroids

Ray Spangenburg and Kit Moser

523.5
SPANGEN
2002

Franklin Watts

A DIVISION OF SCHOLASTIC INC.
NEW YORK · TORONTO · LONDON · AUCKLAND
SYDNEY · MEXICO CITY · NEW DELHI · HONG KONG
DANBURY, CONNECTICUT

For
ANDREA *and* MARK

Photographs © 2002: American Museum of Natural History: 20 (#331042), 47 (#45634); Corbis-Bettmann: 86 (AFP), 53 (Jonathan Blair), 39, 58; Finley-Holiday Films: 22 bottom, 96; Hulton|Archive/Getty Images: 8 (Ali Jarekji/Reuters); Monig Meteorite Collection, Texas Christian University: 38; Museum Victoria, Melbourne, Australia: 82; NASA: 21, 92 (ESA), 42 (Johnson Space Center), 66, 67 (JPL), 24, 34, 45, 50, 55, 72, 79, 85, 104, 111; National Geographic Image Collection/Robert F. Sisson: 63; Photo Researchers, NY: 70, 71, 95, 98 (Julian Baum/SPL), 77 (John Foster), 64 (David A. Hardy/SPL), cover (David Parker/SPL), 60, 61 (Pekka Parviainen/SPL), 19 (Rev. Ronald Royer/SPL), 33, 35 (SPL), 12, 13, 108 (Jay Stevens/SPL), 31 (D. Van Ravenswaay/SPL), 2 (Frank Zullo); Stocktrek: 28; Visuals Unlimited: 14, 103 (Dennis Di Cicco); Yerkes Observatory/University of Chicago: 22 top.

The photograph on the cover shows an areal view of the Meteor Crater near Winslow, AZ. The photograph opposite the title page is a photo of the annual Geminid Meteor Shower.

Library of Congress Cataloging-in-Publication Data
Spangenburg, Ray, 1939-
  Meteors, meteorites, and meteoroids / Ray Spangenburg and Kit Moser.
    p. cm. — (Out of this world)
Summary: Explores the mysteries of rocks that travel vast distances through space, sometimes passing through Earth's atmosphere and sometimes landing on the surface. Includes bibliographical references and index.
  ISBN 0-531-11925-4 (lib. bdg.)   0-531-15567-6 (pbk.)
  1. Meteors—Juvenile literature. 2. Meteorites—Juvenile literature. 3. Meteoroids—Juvenile literature. [1. Meteors. 2. Meteorites. 3. Meteoroids.] I. Moser, Diane, 1944- II. Title. III. Out of this world (Franklin Watts, Inc.)
  QB741.5 .S63 2002
  523.5'1—dc21
                              2002000017

FRANKLIN WATTS and associated logos are trademarks and or registered trademarks of Grolier Publishing Co., Inc. SCHOLASTIC and associated logos are trademarks and or registered trademarks of Scholastic Inc.

1 2 3 4 5 6 7 8 9 10 R 11 10 09 08 07 06 05 04 03 02

Acknowledgments

To all those who have contributed to *Meteors, Meteorites, and Meteoroids,* we would like to take this opportunity to say thank you, with special appreciation to our editor, Melissa Palestro, who has shown both great patience and courage. We would also like to give credit to Melissa Stewart, whose originality and vision provided the initial sparks for this series. Additionally, we would like to thank Sam Storch, lecturer at the American Museum of Natural History–Hayden Planetarium; Margaret W. Carruthers, planetary geologist, Oxford, England; and Dr. Richard Ash, meteoriticist at Oxford University and the Natural History Museum in London, who all reviewed the manuscript and saved the day with many insightful suggestions. If any inaccuracies remain, the fault is ours, not theirs. Finally, many thanks to Tony Reichhardt and John Rhea, our editors at the former *Space World Magazine,* who first started us out on these fascinating journeys into the regions of space, space science, and technology.

Contents

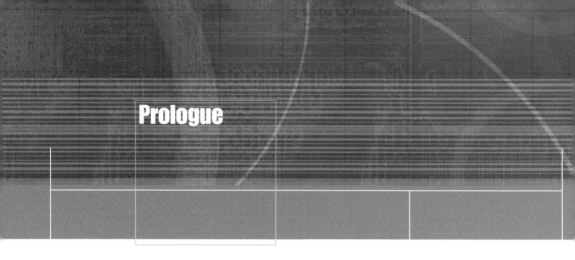

Space Rocks!

The solar system is an exciting, lively place. We know it as a family of planets, moons, and other objects orbiting the Sun and as home to our Earth. But not everyone knows that the solar system has an amazing history full of explosions, collisions, and phenomena so amazing that no special effects in a movie could ever mimic them. What's more, a lot of these events are still going on today.

Space rocks—more formally known as *meteoroids*—play an important part in all this action. Meteoroids are leftovers from the earliest history of the solar system. They range from huge chunks of rock that are bigger than houses to tiny pebbles. For scientists, they are like jagged pieces of a giant puzzle because they may hold the answers to many questions about the formation of the solar system and its early history.

Meteoroids travel in *orbits* around the Sun, as do most objects in the solar system. They don't always stay in their orbits, though. Hundreds and sometimes even thousands of meteoroids fall toward Earth every day, pushed and pulled out of their orbits by collisions and encounters in space. At the same time, they are pulled in by our planet's *gravity.* Most of these meteoroids are very small. Many are so small that, once they smack into Earth's *atmosphere,* they disintegrate rapidly and form bursts of light called *meteors.*

Some of the larger meteoroids do not disappear. They plunge all the way to Earth's surface—pieces of the universe literally "dropping in for a visit." These rocks—the ones that make their way to the surface—

Leonid meteors light up the night sky of the al-Azraq desert in Jordan.

are called *meteorites*. As meteoroids, they traveled vast distances through the solar system before landing on our doorstep. Many are made up of the *primordial* materials from which the planets, moons, asteroids, and comets first formed. Therefore, scientists often find clues in their rocky structures. Scientists have found that many meteorites can provide new information about the history of the solar system.

Recently, scientists discovered that an intense "rain of ice and fire" early in Earth's history may have carried more than ice, fire, and rock to our planet. These early meteorites may have brought the building blocks from which life on Earth developed. Many scientists believe that meteorites hold important clues to how life began.

This book tells the story of the group of small to medium-size "space rocks" known as meteoroids and their other forms, meteors and meteorites. It follows the path of meteoroids that plunge into Earth's atmosphere, the brilliant trail they trace as meteors, and their often explosive arrivals as meteorites on Earth's surface. It explores these mysterious stones from space—what they are, where they come from, where and how we find them, and the secrets we hope to learn from them.

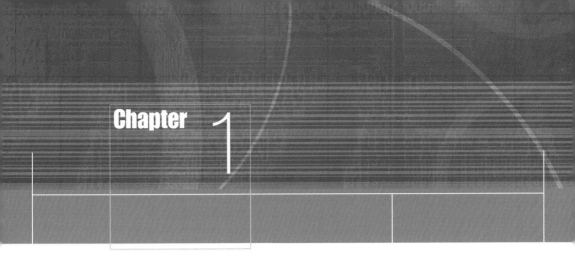

Chapter 1

Meteors: Nature's Fireworks

When you look up at the nighttime sky, you may sometimes notice sudden, bright arcs of light that zip into view and then disappear. Some people call them "falling stars" or "shooting stars," but they are not actually stars at all. They are meteors—the fiery trails of pieces of dust or pebbles that crash into the molecules of Earth's atmosphere. These brightly glowing streaks are caused by friction between the tiny objects and the gases surrounding our planet.

You may have heard that, beyond Earth, space is a vacuum—completely empty space with no air, dust, or anything—interrupted only

A false-color photograph of
a Leonid meteor shower.

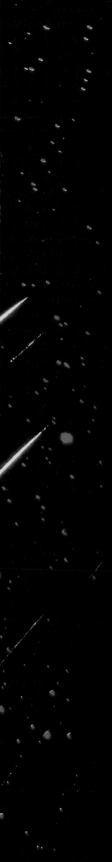

by the objects known as planets, moons, stars (including our Sun), asteroids, and comets. This is not a completely true picture. Space *is* a vacuum, but it is filled with dust particles, gases, and rocks both large and small.

As Earth orbits the Sun, our planet runs into millions of tiny micrometeoroids every day. Micrometeoroids are moving fast when compared to Earth, traveling toward our planet at a rate of 6 to 45 miles (10 to 70 kilometers) per second! The meteoric spectacle begins at the point where Earth's atmosphere becomes thick enough to start interacting with the surfaces of the meteoroid—about 37 miles (60 km) above the ground.

What's in a Name?

How are meteors, meteorites, and meteoroids related? These three names are really just different ways of classifying space rocks and depend upon where you find them. If the space rocks are roaming between the planets—usually orbiting the Sun themselves—they are meteoroids. A meteoroid is any small, extraterrestrial, solid body floating in space. Meteoroids are usually chunks that have broken off from larger bodies in the solar system. A giant *asteroid* (a large space rock orbiting the Sun) may have slammed into another asteroid, causing chips of rock to careen into space. An asteroid may have collided with the Moon or Mars and chipped off pieces that shot into space.

Meteoroids may be tiny—smaller than a grain of rice. Most are smaller than about 0.6 mile (1 km) in *diameter.*

Comet Kobayashi-Berger-Milon was discovered in July 1975 by comet hunter Toru Kobayashi of Japan and confirmed the next day by U.S. amateur astronomers Doug Berger and Dennis Milon. A comet is a rocky ball of ice thought to originate in the outer solar system. Its long orbit extends inward, past the Sun, and the Sun's energy vaporizes the comet's ice, producing a bright, showy tail as it slowly moves against the backdrop of stars.

When an interplanetary object is larger than that, it is usually called either an asteroid or a *comet,* depending on its orbit and history.

A meteoroid becomes a meteor as soon as it falls toward our planet and enters Earth's atmosphere. The word "meteor" refers to both the space rock itself during transit and the blaze of light that many people call a "falling star." Of course, it's not really a star at all. It's just the bright light from a hot, brightly glowing space rock as it collides with gas molecules in Earth's atmosphere.

Most meteors disintegrate before they even come close to Earth's surface. However, some don't. Some smash into Earth and explode on impact, or they explode just before impact. When that happens, remaining fragments of the original meteoroid may be flung onto the ground or buried deep in the soil. These fragments are called mete-orites. So once a space rock hits Earth's surface, it is called a meteorite.

The study of meteors, meteorites, and meteoroids is known as meteoritics. Scientists involved in meteoritics (*meteoriticists*) look at questions such as: Where did these samples originally come from? How do they relate to other bodies in the solar system? Were they formed when the solar system was formed (that is, are they primordial samples)? Or were they formed more recently? Even more important, how did planets form? How long did that process take? Many mete-orites are chips of the planet Mars or the Moon. What can these chunks of rock tell us about the geology of these two neighbors? Why are they different from Earth? Scientists use information they gain from meteorites and translate it into information about the early solar system. The rocks of Earth have all been changed by the many forces at work on our planet's surface, including erosion. So Earth is not a good source for much of the information we would like to know about the solar system's history. The geology of meteorites, however, can remain virtually unchanged over billions of years.

Life Story of a Meteor

As we have explained, a meteor is really the light you see from Earth when a meteoroid enters the atmosphere and begins to heat up. The light is produced when a speeding meteoroid smacks into the gas molecules surrounding Earth, and heats up.

What exactly happens to cause that light to appear? In space, a meteoroid may be traveling at a rate as high as 45 miles (70 km) per second. As it approaches Earth, its speed becomes even greater under the influence of Earth's gravitational field. Any object entering Earth's atmosphere has built up an impressive amount of *kinetic energy*—the energy of motion. As it plunges toward Earth, the meteoroid jostles the atmosphere's gas molecules and friction occurs. The *friction* converts the space rock's kinetic energy into intense, glowing heat.

High in the atmosphere the gas molecules are far apart, so there is time for the heat to radiate away. Lower in the atmosphere the gas molecules are closer together and the rock cannot get rid of the heat that is created. Friction begins to heat the rock and the air around it. This heat starts to melt and then vaporize the surface material of the meteoroid. The surrounding atmospheric gas breaks up into *ions,* or electrically charged particles. As these changes take place, the atoms of both the meteoroid and the atmosphere become even more excited. The result is a large, bright, luminous cloud—a meteor—traveling rapidly across the sky. As the space rock plunges still lower into Earth's atmosphere, a shock wave may develop in the atmosphere ahead of it.

Small meteoroids disappear quickly. They vaporize or burn up completely as they plunge through the outer regions of the atmosphere. This happens for two reasons. The first is a process called *ablation.* The surface molecules of the meteoroid vaporize or turn into molten droplets. Layer by layer, the meteoroid is quickly worn away. Second, the air molecules can't get out of the way fast enough, so they pile up in front of the meteor. The pressure from these molecules crushes the body of the meteoroid, and large fragments break off. Many meteoroids crumble high in the atmosphere, at an altitude of about 50 miles (80 km). Very few get even as low as 30 miles (50 km). Their shows are over in just a few seconds.

So the vast majority of meteors never really get close to Earth. They put on a glorious show, especially when they fall in large numbers. They also show one of the ways our atmosphere protects us—by stopping many incoming objects before they ever reach the surface of the planet.

Some falling space rocks do manage to enter the lower altitudes of Earth's atmosphere. These are usually traveling at slower speeds. They may also be large, but some are very small. Some make their way all the way to Earth's surface and may be recovered as meteorites. The atmosphere usually brings these falling rocks almost to free-fall speed at an altitude of about 3 to 15 miles (5 to 25 km). They cool off, stop glowing, and fall to Earth at a relatively slow speed—about 325 to 650 feet (100 to 200 meters) per second. This part of the trip is sometimes known as the dark flight and can take several minutes.

Some quickly traveling meteors can also be very noisy. Shock waves in the atmosphere can sweep toward the ground, causing loud, rolling sounds like thunder or sonic booms. Most frequently, there follows a whistling sound and a dull thud. In either case, the impact is usually so anticlimatic that no one ever finds the meteorite because no one actually saw where it landed.

One note: Meteors don't exist on bodies in space that have little or no atmosphere, such as the Moon, Mercury, or Jupiter's moon Callisto. An astronaut on the surface of the Moon would never see a shooting star race across the horizon. When a meteoroid speeds toward the Moon, it encounters no gas molecules. There is no atmosphere, so there is no friction—and no bright light from the excited glow of interacting ions. There is nothing to slow the object, either. A space rock on a collision course with the Moon goes barreling in and then smacks it hard. Meteorites hit the surface and dig huge craters. So no one on the Moon has ever seen a meteor cross the sky, and no one ever will.

Showering Meteors

One-at-a-time meteors—or *sporadic meteors*—may show up on any night of the year in any part of the sky. But sometimes, the sky lights up with hundreds—even hundreds of thousands—of showering lights, known as *meteor showers.*

Since ancient times, astronomers have had a system for identifying regions of the nighttime skies. At different times of the year, as Earth moves through its revolution around the Sun, different star groups, or *constellations,* come into view. When you look at the sky during a meteor shower, all the meteors seem to be coming from the same point—a region of the sky astronomers call the *radiant point.* For reference, astronomers name each shower after the star or constellation that seems to be closest to its radiant point. For example, in recent

This photo shows a Perseid meteor shower. The Perseids reach their peak about August 12 each year.

years astronomers noticed that a series of meteor showers usually occurs every year around August 11–12, a time when the constellation Perseus comes into view. The meteors' radiant point seems to be in the area of Perseus. So astronomers have named these showers the Perseid meteor showers.

The meteors are not falling out of the constellation Perseus at all, of course. That is an optical illusion. The stars that make up Perseus are located far, far outside the solar system, many *light-years* away. (A light-year is equal to the distance light travels in a year.) The meteors are traveling side by side in the space surrounding Earth. They seem to be falling straight toward us from a single point in the sky because of an illusion of perspective. It is similar to the illusion that you see when you stand between parallel railroad tracks and look into the distance. The tracks appear to meet at a "vanishing point" near the horizon.

Long ago, astronomers noticed that these big meteor showers seemed to occur on regular schedules. For a long time, no one could imagine why meteor showers should take place on a schedule. Even more confusing was the fact that not all of these schedules were annual. Some occurred at much longer intervals, often several years apart.

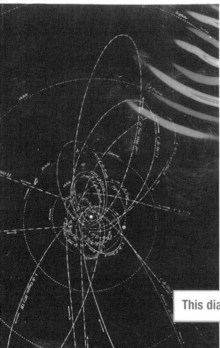

This diagram shows the orbits of comets around the Sun.

The Comet Connection

Comets are nothing like meteors. Astronomers like to call comets "dirty snowballs" because they are composed mostly of ice and a little bit of rock. A comet seems to move slowly across the sky because it is so far away. It does not come close to Earth and its atmosphere unless it has an Earth-crossing orbit. Astronomers think that most comets come either from the *Kuiper Belt* just beyond Pluto or from a region known as the *Oort cloud* at the outer edge of the solar system. Many comets have very long, *highly eccentric* orbits that stretch inward toward the Sun from points billions of miles away. A comet may take many hundreds of years to return to the region of the inner solar system where observers on Earth can catch a glimpse of it.

When a comet does arrive in the inner solar system, observers can watch it from night to night as it makes its way toward the Sun. A fuzzy streak of bright light trails behind it as it passes into the inner solar system and approaches the Sun's heat and radiation. This streak

You probably recognize Edmond Halley (1656–1742) as the astronomer after whom Halley's comet is named. Halley began observing stars earnestly in 1676 at the age of twenty. That was the year he set off for the southern hemisphere to begin making a record of the stars he could see from that region of Earth's surface. Until then, all European and British astronomers had recorded observations only from north of the equator, where the skies look entirely different from the skies in the southern hemisphere. Seamen and travelers had made some observations south of the equator, but otherwise, Halley was the first northern astronomer in the region.

Halley traveled to the South Atlantic and established the first southern observatory on the island of St. Helena. The weather turned out to be poor for astronomy on St. Helena, but he managed to record 341 stars in two years. He returned to England as a hero among astronomers. The Royal Society, England's prestigious scientific association,

Edmond Halley.

elected him to membership. He was only twenty-two years old.

Halley became a good friend of Isaac Newton (1642–1727) in 1684, and the two scientists worked together to figure out how comets move. To seventeenth-century astronomers, comets seemed to be the outlaws of the skies. They seemed to appear and then disappear, as if they were just "passing through" the sky without coming back into view the way the planets and the Moon did.

Halley first saw the comet we call Halley's comet in 1682. When he looked at astronomical records, he noticed something interesting: It was following the same path as a comet that passed through the sky in 1456, 1531, and 1607. The four comets had appeared just 75 to 76 years apart. Halley had a bright idea: Maybe all four were the same comet!

In 1705 Halley predicted that his comet would return in 1758. He didn't get to see it happen, but he was right. It also returned in 1835 and 1910. Thanks to Halley, scientists now know that comets travel in orbits, just as Earth, the planets, and the Moon do. They are just much longer *ellipses*. The most recent visit to the Sun by Halley's comet in 1986 allowed spacecraft to get within 376 miles (605 km) of the comet to get the first close-up view ever.

An artist's depiction of Halley's comet.

is a trail of vaporized ice and gas shimmering in the sunlight that is pushed away from the Sun by the *solar wind.*

So what is the connection between comets and meteors? As a comet approaches, the Sun's heat vaporizes the ice. Particles of dust and chunks of rock break off from the cracks and fissures that form. A comet may have many craters and jagged edges that mark areas where chunks have broken off. These chunks and particles of dust lag behind, following along in the comet's orbit. If the comet crosses Earth's orbit, it leaves some of those clumps of material behind, right in Earth's path. So as Earth makes its way along its own orbital path around the Sun, it may encounter many micrometeoroids for several years following a comet's visit. Since the material may remain floating in the same part of Earth's orbit for a long time, the Earth encounters this cometary trail at the same time every year, when the same constellation is in view. That's why we have patterns of annual meteor showers.

Spectacular Showers

Every now and then, a meteor shower can be not only beautiful but sensational—a sky lit up with dazzling fireworks. A woodcut illustration created after the great Leonid meteor shower that occurred in 1833 looks like an extraordinary exaggeration. People are looking up in amazement from the streets of a small town as literally thousands of lights shower down from the nighttime sky. Surely the artist got carried away! Yet reports of the event back up the accuracy of the artist's representation.

The Leonid meteor shower of 1833 prompted astronomical historians to go back in the records of meteor showers to see if they could see a pattern. They found accounts of about twenty-eight spectacular

This is a contemporary artist's vision of the 1833 Leonid meteor shower.

meteor showers between the years 902 and 1833. All twenty-eight, they discovered, took place when the constellation Leo was high in the sky. These twenty-eight events occurred regularly, 33 years apart, and always at the same time of year. Would 1866 be another big year? Astronomers thought so, and they were right! Between 1899 and 1966, the Leonid showers tapered off. Then, in 1966, the Leonids made a sensational return.

"It was a night I will never forget," wrote one astronomer. The sky was filled with so many "falling stars" that counting them was impossible. They were everywhere in the sky and falling fast. Estimates of the numbers reached 150,000 meteors in the three hours just before dawn. Sky watchers had high hopes for another brilliant show in 1999, but by comparison it was disappointing.

Another sensational twentieth-century meteor shower took place in 1946. On October 9, Earth passed through debris left behind by the comet Giacobini-Zinner when it crossed Earth's orbit. The night was not dark—a full moon made the fainter meteors difficult to see. Yet the sky filled with as many as two hundred meteors an hour. Because the bright showers seemed to radiate from the constellation Draco, these meteors are called the Draconids. The comet's debris seems to have decreased, and the glorious show of 1946 has not been repeated in recent years.

Many astronomers recommend watching the Perseid showers, though. A Perseid shower takes place yearly between August 9 and August 12, and counts usually run as high as sixty meteors an hour. Viewing is improved if the Moon is not full—and of course, all sky watching is better if you can get away from city lights. A little patience also helps!

Meteor Showers
Vital Statistics

Name	Time of Year	Comet
QUARANTID	January 2–4	Not known
LYRID	April 21–22	Thatcher (1861 I)
ETA AQUARID	May 3–5	Halley
PERSEID	August 11–12	Swift-Tuttle
DRACONID	October 8–9	Giacobini-Zinner
ORIONID	October 20–21	Halley
TAURID	November 7–8	Encke
LEONID	November 16–17	Tempel-Tuttle
URSID	December 22	Mechain-Tuttle

Fireballs

The material from comets that showers into the atmosphere in cycles rarely reaches Earth's surface. However, sometimes other space rocks do. These objects are primarily fractured pieces of iron and other rock that have been knocked off asteroids by collisions. Their sizes range from about the size of a golf ball to the size of a compact automobile.

An impact from one of these space rocks may be preceded by an extremely bright descent through the atmosphere, called a *fireball*. These brilliant streaks can light up the sky as brightly as the Moon, and some rival the brightness of the Sun.

When a fairly large incoming meteoroid enters the atmosphere traveling at cosmic speed, it heats up quickly. The stony outer layer melts into a thin, glassy skin. A large surrounding area of gases becomes heated to high temperatures and begins to glow very brightly. This crown surrounding the speeding rock makes the object look both a lot bigger and closer to Earth than it really is.

As the fireball approaches Earth, aerodynamic pressure increases. If the incoming rock has fractures or its structure is unstable in other ways, it may break up and scatter into a train of brightly lit objects trailing behind the main fireball. A fireball that explodes before hitting Earth's surface is often referred to as a *bolide*. (You may see the word "bolide" used more loosely to describe any fireball, especially in older information sources.)

The Hazardous Side

Observers certainly must have noticed these eerie fireworks displays from the beginning of human existence. Young people have probably watched "falling stars" for thousands and thousands of years.

Yet not all meteor falls are quite so unmenacing. A harsh reminder of the power of an incoming space rock was delivered in 1908. A meteor soared through the skies over central Siberia at about 8 on the morning of June 30. It was the brightest meteor ever recorded and lit up the sky as brightly as the Sun does. A third of the way around the world, a woman in London looked out her window and could see an eerie, bright red glow along the eastern horizon, which was still dark because the Sun had not yet risen in England.

No one is quite certain what happened next. Apparently, the fireball exploded before it hit the ground. The explosion was as powerful as a 10-megaton thermonuclear bomb. More than 725 square miles (1,878 square kilometers) of forest were flattened. Tall trees were blasted to the ground like toothpicks. The explosion occurred near the Tunguska River—a sparsely populated wilderness region. A few herdsmen camping nearby with their herd of reindeer were the only eyewitnesses. If an explosion such as this one had occurred in a more populated area, the loss of human life and property would have been enormous. Fortunately, impacts the size of the Tunguska event are rare.

These trees were knocked flat and stripped bare by the Tunguska explosion of 1908.

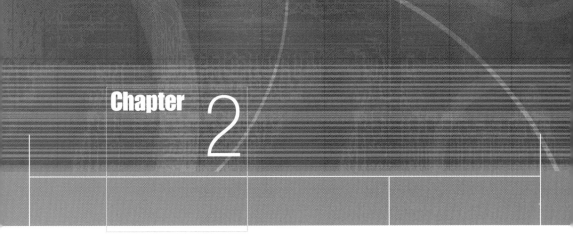

Chapter 2

Meteorites: Rocks From the Sky

o you remember the story of Chicken Little? In the story, the silly little chicken thought the sky was falling when someone threw a star-shaped chunk of wood at him. Well, Chicken Little did have a silly idea—the sky is not a hard object that can fall on you. However, as you know, pieces of the solar system can and do fall to Earth from space. It's an idea that doesn't sound quite right somehow, and rocks that fell from the sky really puzzled people from ancient times until the early twentieth century!

Ancient Legends

"Stones from the sky" turn up in the earliest writings from China, Rome, and Greece. Often, ancient people collected these rocks and built sacred shrines around them.

According to Roman records, generals undertook an attack to seize a meteorite enshrined in a temple in Turkey around 220 B.C. They thought the rock had powers that would help them defend Roman territories against the invading general Hannibal. (No records show that any advantage was gained, however.)

In a sacred Muslim legend, a special black rock was given to Ishmael (son of Abraham) by the Angel Gabriel. Since before Muhammad's conquest of Mecca around A.D. 600, the Black Stone has been located in Mecca in the Kaaba, Islam's most important shrine. For centuries the Black Stone has been the most venerated object in the Muslim community. Some accounts indicate that the Black Stone may be a meteorite, since it is both black and heavy, two common features of meteorites. However, another account claims that the Black Stone floats—which a meteorite definitely would not do. Without further examination, it is unclear what type of rock it is.

The much-respected Greek philosopher Aristotle fought against the idea that rocks could fall from the heavens. Could that happen, since the heavenly bodies were perfect, wondered Aristotle? Also, rocks were made in Earth's interior, he said. Therefore, how could they come from above? His point of view was challenged by nature in 467 B.C. when witnesses saw a large rock fall in nearby Thrace, in what is now the southeastern Balkan Peninsula. Still unconvinced that the rock came from the heavens, Aristotle concluded that it must have been swept up into the air from the ground by unusually strong winds. This was a very unlikely conclusion, but it was a conclusion that fit well into Aristotle's view of the world.

The world's oldest surviving witnessed meteorite fell on May 19, 861, at Nogata, Japan. Today it resides in a Shinto Buddhist shrine. Similar events occurred in other parts of the world. On November 7, 1492, villagers near Ensisheim in Alsace (now part of France) heard a loud explosion. A 280-pound (130-kilogram) meteorite had streaked out of the sky and put a large dent in a local wheat field. Its fall is recorded in a woodcut illustration made in that year. The woodcut is still preserved in a library in Tübingen, Germany. In this picture, the big, angular object descends from the cloudy skies and streaks toward the hillside near Ensisheim and its castle. Jagged lines accompany the rock as it tumbles from the sky, and two figures watch cautiously from the corner of the picture. Historical documents tell of only one boy, though, who saw the fall. He took villagers to the wheat field, where the big rock had dug a hole 3 feet (1m) deep.

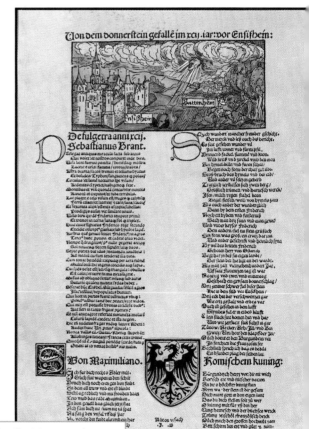

This medieval manuscript page was the first to record a meteorite. The top of the page shows a woodcut depicting the meteorite that fell near Ensisheim on November 7, 1492.

The villagers and townspeople were in awe and believed that the rock had supernatural importance. Many took samples and souvenirs until the town magistrate ordered its protection.

When King Maximilian of Germany rode through the area, the rock gained political importance. He proclaimed that the frightening event showed God's anger against the French, who were warring against Maximilian and the Holy Roman Empire. By Maximilian's order, the rock went on display in the village church as a reminder that God was on his side. There it was preserved until the French Revolution three centuries later, when it was confiscated for a national museum at Colmar. Scientists took samples at that time for testing, and numerous museums around the world have some of these samples. Today, a large piece of the meteorite resides in a museum at Ensisheim—much reduced and rounded by centuries of sampling. It is still heavy though—120 pounds (55 kg). You wouldn't want that to fall on your head! It is 15.75 inches (40 centimeters) in diameter.

In spite of the attention the Ensisheim meteorite received when it fell, later scientists were reluctant to believe that the rock had fallen from the heavens. There was apparently only one witness, and it had happened long ago.

In 1751 a large meteorite *fall* was reported by people living in Zagreb, now in Croatia. The bishop of Zagreb collected the pieces and gathered accounts told by witnesses. He considered the event historically important and sent the rocks and stories he had gathered to the emperor of Austria. From there, the collection was sent to a Vienna museum. However, the museum gave the collection no attention at the time.

Most scientists in the 1700s were very skeptical about accounts of rocks falling from the sky. They thought these stories were hysterical fables—tales told by ignorant peasants with overactive imaginations. In fact, the word "meteor," from the Greek term *meteron,* originally had no connection with the idea of rocks falling to Earth from space. It meant just an airborne object or a phenomenon that took place in the skies. That's why meteorology is the study of the weather and has nothing to do with meteors, meteorites, or meteoroids!

In 1794 a German physicist and lawyer named Ernest F.F. Chladni published a study he performed of some of these "stones from the sky." One of the rocks had been picked up after a fireball sighting. Chladni was the first to figure out that these rocks came from space, and he said so in his report. He even suggested the possibility that they were chunks of a planet that had broken up.

Chladni's work was almost completely rejected at first by other scientists. His evidence was strong and he presented it carefully, yet the idea just didn't fit with what "seemed right" at the time.

Another study came out in 1796. Finally, this paper accepted the idea that rocks could fall from the sky. But now, as did Aristotle, the argument stated that tornadoes had swept them up into the atmosphere from the ground, and from there they fell back to Earth. The study still resisted the idea that rocks on Earth could come from outer space.

Then, on January 1, 1801, the astronomer Giuseppe Piazzi discovered the first asteroid. It turned out to be the largest asteroid in existence. Ceres had a diameter of 623 miles

Giuseppe Piazzi.

Jupiter and its four largest moons, shown in a montage.

(1,003 km) and is located in what is now known as the *Main Asteroid Belt*—a wide region between Jupiter and Mars where thousands of asteroids follow independent orbits around the Sun. Until the discovery of Ceres, no one knew anything about any celestial objects smaller than a moon. (And most moons known at that time were the largest of the satellites, such as Jupiter's moons Ganymede and Callisto and Saturn's moon, Titan.) The discovery of smaller objects—even one several miles wide, such as Ceres—made Chladni's ideas about rocks originating from space seem a lot more plausible.

One of the strongest groups that opposed the idea of meteorites was the French Academy of Sciences. This group of scientists refused to accept the importance of the peasants' reports and rock collections. Finally, though, they had to pay attention. On April 26, 1803, a large meteorite broke into a shower of fragments over the French town of L'Aigle. The Academy decided to send a scout to see the rocks in person, so they picked a renowned physicist named Jean-Baptiste Biot. When he arrived in L'Aigle, Biot found and collected about 17 pounds (8 kg) of small rocks that had fallen to Earth on that date. His evidence was carefully documented and his reputation as a scientist was excellent. Finally, the scientific world was convinced that rocks do fall from the sky.

Even after Biot's careful work, though, scientists across the Atlantic in the United States remained skeptical. After

Jean-Baptiste Biot.

We now know that the scientists who rejected the idea of rocks falling from space were wrong. Does that mean that scientific methods don't work? No. Scientists are human. Sometimes they hold prejudices, just as everyone else does. However, when scientists make decisions based on prejudice and not on the evidence, they are not doing "good science." That is, they are not using scientific methods to arrive at their conclusions. In this case, they were going with what seemed right to them. Unfortunately, most people have a lot of difficulty separating themselves from what they already believe. No matter how hard you try, you tend to see what you want to see, not what is really happening. This fact is a hard obstacle for scientists to overcome, even though objectivity is always their goal.

But let's not be too hard on the eighteenth-century scientists who questioned the stories about falling rocks. At first, the evidence *was* sketchy—and probably sounded a little hysterical. They did not want to look foolish by accepting the observations if they were, indeed, incorrect. What's important is that the scientists did carefully examine the evidence when it was available. They tried to look at the facts objectively. They studied the rocks and the areas where the rocks fell. Finally, even though it didn't sound right at first, they recognized that rocks do fall from space.

Science is not about being right. It's about looking for an accurate description of reality. Real science is "self-correcting." That is, when the gathered facts no longer fit the theories, scientists rewrite their theories.

an explosion in the skies over Weston, Connecticut, in 1807, several rocks plummeted to Earth in the surrounding area. Two scientists from nearby Yale University scoured the area for evidence and found about 330 pounds (150 kg) of rocks. Many witnesses had seen the rocks falling. The scientists were methodical about their collection. Their gathered evidence became the first meteorite collection in the United States, which is still housed at Yale University.

Yet not everyone was convinced. Thomas Jefferson, himself a respected scientist and the president of the country, reportedly remarked, "I would more easily believe that two Yankee professors would lie than that stones would fall from heaven." No one is sure that he actually said that because no original source exists. However, he was very skeptical about rocks falling from the sky.

In a report he wrote about the Weston meteorites, Jefferson cautioned against the "error and misconceptions to which even our senses are liable." He was right. Our own perceptions can fool us. One of the best reasons for using the scientific method is to keep yourself from fooling yourself. Jefferson continued, "It may be difficult to explain how the rock you possess came into the position in which it was found. But is it easier to explain how it got into the clouds from whence it is supposed to have fallen? The actual fact, however, is the thing to be established."

Jefferson was on solid ground. He doubted that the rocks could have been created in the atmosphere and rained down upon Earth. He called for an investigation of the actual facts. Without more information, he wasn't ready to place his bets. Of course, we now know he was both right and wrong. Stony material is not manufactured in the clouds (unless you count hailstones, which are technically rocks made of ice). However, space rocks do fall through the skies and land on Earth.

Witnessing a Fall

Much bigger falls have occurred both before and since the falls at Thrace, Nogata, Ensisheim, L'Aigle, and Weston. As scientists have explored further, they have found several very large meteorites, some weighing several tons. In recent years, new evidence has shown that Earth received some really big impacts in the distant past. And people have experienced several events that have strongly made the point that objects do hit Earth.

One event of this kind occurred on February 18, 1948. A little before 4 P.M., a huge fireball appeared against a clear blue sky over east-central Colorado. It was traveling fast—so fast that no one who spotted it saw it for longer than five seconds. Two airline pilots flying a B-29 saw the enormous ball of fire over Colorado. People in northwestern Kansas and southwestern Nebraska caught sight of it and heard its thundering noise. A thin, trailing line of smoke strung out behind it. Finally, residents of Norton, Kansas, were rocked by a series of tremendous explosions. Buildings shook. People to the west saw the line of smoke broken into a series of clouds. The rapidly traveling space rock apparently broke into smaller chunks in a series of explosions.

A piece of the Norton Meteorite.

Members of the Chinese Academy of Sciences examine the big hole that was made on March 8, 1976, by the Jilin, China, meteorite.

A careful search of the area around Norton turned up several large masses of a type of stony meteorite. Then, about six months later, in the middle of a wheat field, a farmer nearly drove his tractor into a huge, gaping hole that was 10 feet (3 m) deep. At the bottom of the hole was the biggest piece of the meteorite—a massive chunk weighing 2,360 pounds (1,070 kg). It had plowed 10 feet (3 m) into the soft ground. Until 1976 it was the largest meteorite ever recovered from a witnessed fall. Some 4 tons of meteorites fell near Jilin, China, after a witnessed fall on March 8, 1976. At 1.7 tons, the largest recovered rock from that fall surpasses the Norton, Kansas, record. Both falls gained worldwide attention. It certainly has become clear that rocks do fall from space. And sometimes they are big ones!

About 10,000 tons of meteoritic debris reach the surface every year, but most of it is dust. It just sifts down through the atmosphere because its particles are too small to run into much opposition from the atmosphere. But if a meteoroid is going to survive a trip through Earth's atmosphere and land on the surface, it must be either large or hardy, or both, and it can't be traveling too fast. As it falls, it is dazzlingly bright. It produces energetic shock waves that sound like sonic booms because it is traveling at supersonic speed. Throughout history, observers have noticed sounds "like distant guns at sea" or "like a horse and carriage clattering over a bridge" or "like the whomping of helicopter blades." A dusty train of debris stretches behind as layers peel off the speeding meteor. Finally, the rock may fragment, scattering its pieces over its path. It may explode in midair. Or it may crash into the ground, splash into the ocean, or skid across an icy hill.

Hundreds of tons of meteorites fall toward Earth every day. Most of the meteorites are microscopic particles called micrometeorites. An object large enough to hit the ground and cause a crater smacks into Earth about once a year. Big explosions affecting a local area occur about once every hundred years. Catastrophic hits affecting large areas of land take place much more infrequently, about once every 100,000 years.

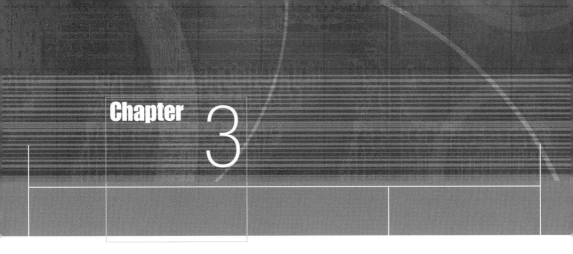

Chapter 3

The Great Hunt

Today, the hunt for rocks from space is exciting and challenging. Scientists now know a lot more about meteorites, where they come from, and what we can learn from them. They come in all sizes and many types. In many ways, each one is unique—and every meteorite recovered is a new opportunity to learn more about the solar system and its history.

What is it like to find a big meteorite fall? Ask Jim Brook, an outdoorsman who found the first pieces of the largest meteorite fall ever recovered in Canada. A spectacular fireball had sped across the sky from the Yukon Territory in northwestern Canada heading south into northern British Columbia. It was the morning of January 18, 2000. Eyewitnesses said the fireball was so brilliant that it lit up the countryside as it sizzled overhead. A few minutes later, the sound waves shook

Three samples of meteorites that fell to Earth. Left: The Allende Meteorite that fell in Mexico in 1969. Center: Sample of the Yukon Meteorite, which exploded over Yukon Territory, Canada, on January 18, 2000. Right: This Murchison Meteorite sample fell to Earth in Australia in 1969.

the ground like a huge explosion. Satellites maintained by the U.S. Department of Defense reported sighting a 440,000-pound (200,000-kg) meteoroid hit the atmosphere. The satellites measured the space rock at about 15 feet (5 m) in diameter.

Eight days later, Brook was driving his truck across the thick ice that covered an arm of Tagish Lake in British Columbia. He noticed some small, dark rocks on the ice. He strongly suspected what they were because, as he explained, "rocks aren't found on the ice, and I could see the outer melted crust."

Darkness ended Brook's search that evening, but the next day he managed to scoop up several dozen space rocks. In the days that followed, researchers from the University of Western Ontario and the University of Calgary, as well as the National Aeronautics and Space Administration (NASA), carefully went over the site Brook had discovered. They found some five hundred tiny pieces of the meteorite and were able to collect several hundred of the fragile fragments. Many of them were still encased in ice when they were recovered.

"This is the *find* of a lifetime," remarked Peter Brown, a meteoriticist who was coleader of the search. "The size of the initial object and the extreme rarity and organic richness of the meteorites, combined with the number we have uncovered, make this a truly unique event."

Many individuals also contributed photos and videos to the researchers' sources for discovering more about the large, fragmented rock. Thanks to this cooperation, including observation by two U.S. defense satellites, scientists were able to calculate both the velocity and the trajectory, or path, of the fireball. From this information they were also able to figure the meteorite's size before it entered the atmosphere, its orbit, and where in space the Tagish Lake meteorite came from.

Could You Find a Meteorite?

Think about the vastness of our planet Earth—millions of square miles of deep oceans, steep mountainsides, shifting desert sands, icy plains, and fertile meadows. How could anyone ever find the chunks of rock and iron that fall from the skies?

The most direct way is to see a space rock falling from the skies and to watch it fall all the way to the ground (without getting hit, of course). In this case, the meteorite is called a fall. When observers can locate the object they saw falling, they already know the date of the fall by direct observation.

Many meteorites are discovered lying on the ground or buried in an ancient crater. These are known as finds.

There are three main classes of meteorites, categorized by their composition, or makeup: irons, stones, and stony-irons. Iron meteorites, or irons, contain about 98 percent nickel-iron. Stones, or stony meteorites, are only about 23 percent nickel-iron, and stony-irons are about 50 percent nickel-iron.

Which of these types of meteorites is most common? That depends on how you're looking at the question. As of 1997, roughly 93 percent of all recorded meteorites were stones and 6 percent were irons. Only about 1 percent were stony-iron meteorites.

Another way of looking at the statistics is this: Which meteorites are the most common finds—meteorites not connected with a fall? Most common of all is a special type of stony meteorite known as a *chondrite*. After chondrites, though, many finds are irons. Why? Iron is less subject to erosion by weathering than the rocky material of the stony and stony-iron meteorites. Also, irons are most easily recognized by amateurs who, like Jim Brook, play a big role in the meteorite hunt.

Many meteorites look a lot like other rocks you might find, but don't let that discourage you. Like Jim Brook, you could find a meteorite that will lead to a new understanding about space rocks, our planet, and the solar system. Finding meteorites is one of the many exciting ways in which amateurs can contribute to the process of science.

Experts offer these basic clues: Look for evidence of melting during the plunge through Earth's atmosphere. If the meteorite fell recently, a formation called a fusion crust may encase the rock in a black, almost glassy film. Look for dark, unusually heavy rocks. The best places to look have little plant growth and light-colored ground. Forested areas or regions with lots of black rocks (such as a lava bed) are poor places to look because it's too hard to spot dark meteorites among all the other objects competing for the searcher's attention.

Take along two tools: a magnet and a magnifying glass. The iron in many meteorites causes them to be attracted to magnets—a quick and easy first test. Then take a look at the shape. As a meteorite plunges through the atmosphere, it encounters forces that tend to round sharp corners. An oblong rock usually becomes an ellipse or a sphere. If the meteorite didn't rotate a lot, one side may form a blunt point with conelike sides. This shape is called oriented. It only develops, though, if the space rock does not tumble as it falls.

Look for signs of impact, fracturing, shock, and weathering that might tell a story of travel in space, a plunge through Earth's atmosphere, and a crash landing. By studying the pictures and descriptions of meteorites in this book, you'll begin to recognize what to look for. Also, look for pictures on the Internet, in other books, and in museums. Then happy hunting! If you find one, take it to the nearest planetarium or report it to the National Museum of Natural History, Department of Mineral Sciences at the Smithsonian Institution in Washington, D.C. Many museums, including the Smithsonian, have programs for authenticating meteorites. They also accept donations for scientific study. Each meteorite is unique and may hold clues about our solar system's past.

This meteorite's black, shiny fusion crust is a sign of melting during passage through Earth's atmosphere.

For falls—meteorites found after they were seen falling—the percentages for irons are still around 6 percent. Stones are much more common among witnessed falls. So scientists conclude that, in space, stony meteoroids are much more common than iron ones.

Shapes and Complexions

Stones are usually fairly smooth, with gentle curves on their surfaces and few pits. They may break on impact, and the fractured areas usually show no signs of heating and are lighter-colored than the exterior.

Irons, however, may be pitted with numerous indentations known as thumbprints—because that's what they look like! Originally, the rock was probably seeded near the surface with small blobs, or nodules, of material that had lower melting points than the surrounding iron. During the heat and friction of the descent, the nodules melted and left behind these strange thumbprints.

Irons also tend to have more angular shapes. A greater percentage of irons are oriented than stones, including a gigantic meteorite found in Oregon's Willamette Valley in 1902. It weighs 15.5 tons and is the largest meteorite ever found in the United States. It measures 4.5 feet (1.37 m) high, 10.25 feet (3.12 m) across the widest part of the base, and 6.5 feet (2 m) across the most narrow part of the base. The enormous rock's conical shape is typical of oriented meteorites. The sides of the cone are fairly smooth, but the base is marked with huge depressions. These resulted when Oregon's wet climate combined rainwater with the meteorite's huge nodules of an *iron sulfide* mineral called troilite. Sulfuric acid formed and etched away the nodules, leaving big basins and cavities in the meteorite.

The Willamette Meteorite.

Irons commonly have sharp edges caused by fragmenting that occurs on impact or during descent. The roughest exteriors are found on stony-iron meteorites, though—especially if they are composed of a network of iron filled with *olivine* crystals. Olivine is less resistant to weathering and may weather out of the rock, leaving a coarse texture on the meteorite.

One day in 1902, an Oregon farmer named Ellis Hughes was cutting wood in the forest near his farm when he noticed a gigantic rock. It was huge and bell-shaped, and the ground around it was slightly depressed. Hughes quickly realized that it was a meteorite and that it could be a great tourist attraction. He and his wife decided to move the giant meteorite from where he found it—on property belonging to the Oregon Iron and Steel Company—to his own property. Of course, this plan wasn't legal. A meteorite belongs to the owner of the property on which it is found. Moreover, the Clackamas tribe, who had lived in the region longer than anyone else, had a long history of prior ownership of the meteorite.

(By the way, if you're wondering why Hughes didn't find the meteorite at the bottom of a huge crater, you're asking a good question. Some scientists think the meteorite originally fell in Canada and was carried south by a huge glacier during the last Ice Age.)

Hughes devised a complicated system of *capstans,* cables, an old horse, and a sturdy wagon. Through great effort, he succeeded in moving the meteorite. What he overlooked, though, was the evidence he left behind. He had cleared a path through the thick forest, along which he carted the rock onto his own property. Investigators easily discovered the trail, so Hughes's profits from his undertaking were short-lived.

After many court battles, Oregon Iron and Steel won custody of the meteorite and displayed it at the Lewis and Clark World's Fair in Portland. In 1906 the company sold it for $26,000, and today you can see the Willamette Meteorite on display at the American Museum of Natural History in New York City.

In June 2000, the museum signed an agreement with the Confederated Tribes of the Grand Ronde, the elected government of the Clackamas tribe. The museum recognized the cultural importance of the meteorite to the Clackamas. According to tribal legend, the great rock was Tomanowos, a powerful representative of the Sky People. When Tomanowos arrived on Earth, earth, sky, and water were united. As a result of the agreement, the tribal peoples now have access to the meteorite at the museum for annual cultural celebrations, and the museum gets to keep this rare scientific object on display, as it has for nearly a century.

Fool's Meteorites?

Unfortunately, identifying a meteorite is not always easy. Many terrestrial rocks are also pitted, dark, and dense. One Earth rock that people often mistake for a meteorite is an ore called magnetite. It is an iron-oxide *ore* (iron that has combined with oxygen) that is often found in the desert. Like an iron meteorite, it is attracted to a magnet. However, magnetite leaves a black streak when you rub it on a hard surface. A meteorite usually doesn't because its exterior is glassy because of the heat it endured during its trip through the atmosphere.

Terrestrial rocks that have been tumbled and rounded by water can sometimes be mistaken for meteorites. Sometimes, a mineral stain builds up on the outside of these rocks so they appear dark on the outside and light on the inside—a lot like a stony meteorite with a fusion crust.

The dark chunks of residue left over from coal furnaces, metal manufacturing, and mining sometimes look like meteorites, too. Also, people sometimes think they have found a meteorite when it is just a tektite. A tektite is a type of rock formed from ordinary Earth rocks during an impact. The heat of the impact turned the rocks into molten blobs that later hardened. A tektite may be caused by a meteorite hit, but it is not actually a "rock from the sky."

Real meteorites come in many shapes, kinds, and sizes. Some are tiny—the size of a pinhead or smaller across. Some are much bigger, and when they started out as meteoroids, before entering Earth's atmosphere, they may have been up to a mile (1.6 km) in diameter. (If they are any bigger, they are usually called asteroids, but this is by no means a hard-and-fast rule.) Where in the solar system they have traveled and what happened to them before they arrived on Earth varies. And many of them have been lying on Earth's surface for thousands or even millions of years.

Many meteorites have undergone changes after entering Earth's atmosphere. These changes are caused by the heat, pressure, and mechanical shock of their passage and landing. In some cases, the heating is not extreme and the space rock's characteristics may have been altered only slightly. Some are severely altered by melting; then they become solid again as a lavalike rock or metal.

Scientists have used the variety of differentiation to classify meteorites. This method also provides clues about what kind of parent bodies these rocks came from and what happened to them during their history.

Crystals of brown olivine and white pyroxene occur throughout this cross-section of the Martian meteorite ALH77005. The sample also shows gray areas that once melted during an impact. The cube at right in the photo provides size comparison. It measures .39 inches (1 cm).

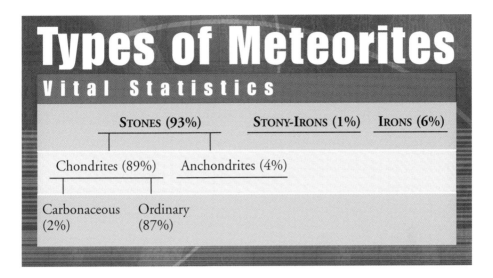

Types of Meteorites

Vital Statistics

STONES (93%)		STONY-IRONS (1%)	IRONS (6%)
Chondrites (89%)	Anchondrites (4%)		
Carbonaceous (2%)	Ordinary (87%)		

Irons Up Close

Iron meteorites come primarily from the *core* of some other world. When the planets, asteroids, and moons were molten during the early days of the solar system, melted iron was the heaviest element. So the melted iron accumulated at the center of these objects and formed their cores. Iron meteorites were almost certainly formed by the cataclysmic impacts of objects with asteroids. The cores of objects cannot be shattered by gentle, grazing bumps from other objects because they are protected by the outer layers of materials. The bodies of these asteroids must be completely destroyed.

Iron meteorites resist weathering and erosion better than other meteorites. They also do not break easily. So the largest meteorites found are usually irons. The composition of iron meteorites may give scientists some insight into the composition of Earth's own core.

Scientists use a system of classification for irons that is based on the presence of *siderophile elements,* a group of elements that is attracted to metals. These elements include germanium, gallium, osmium, and iridium.

Meteoriticists use a structural scheme for classifying irons. They divide iron meteorites into three main types: hexahedrites, octahedrites, and ataxites. Each of these structures reflects the amount of nickel in the meteorite's nickel-iron alloy and how quickly the material it came from cooled.

The first type, hexahedrites, contains large, cubic crystals of kamacite, a type of nickel-iron alloy. The second type, octahedrites, contains two types of nickel-iron alloys, kamacite and taenite. The third type, ataxites, appears to have no internal structure. Irons may also have additional elements embedded within them. These are called *inclusions.* The large holes and pits that are so common in iron meteorites may originally have been resting places for graphite nodules. Graphite is a form of carbon commonly found in irons. However, it is also easily ablated away.

Stony-Irons—Simple Combinations

If iron meteorites can be thought of as the cores of asteroids or other objects that have been blasted apart, then stony-irons can be thought of as originating from the mantles of these objects. Stony-irons have melted at some time in the past and have recrystallized.

Stony-irons seem to be rare in space. Less than 3 percent of all known meteorites are stony-irons. Scientists have given them three classifications: the pallasites, the mesosiderites, and the lodranites. Pallasites are made up primarily of nickel-iron with nodules of olivine. Mesosiderites and lodranites (which are very uncommon) combine aggregates of nickel-iron with other minerals.

Meteorite collector Robert Haag holds a beautiful sample of a pallasite meteorite. This meteorite type contains areas of olivine (lighter areas) distributed throughout a network of iron-nickel metal (darker areas).

Stony Meteorites—A Varied Family

Stones are the most common meteorites of all. They are basically pieces of crust from a planet, a moon, or an asteroid. Because the crust wraps around the outside of an object, it is the most easily knocked off, so the plentiful supply of these meteorites is no surprise.

Most stony meteorites contain interesting formations known as *chondrules* (from a Greek word meaning "seed grain"). Chondrules are small, BB-size, glassy balls, or *spherules*. Scientists think chondrules may have formed during the melting of materials that took place during the formation of the solar system. During this period, many objects collided with each other, and the impacts caused extreme heating.

The class of stony meteorites in which these tiny spheres are found is called chondrites. Scientists think that chondrite meteorites probably formed very early, making them some of the most primitive objects in the solar system. When these primordial objects fall to Earth, they provide a superb opportunity for scientists to find out about the early history of Earth, the other planets, and their moons.

A much smaller group of stones have no chondrules, so they are called *achondrites* (the prefix "a-" means "without"). These make up only about 4 percent of all stony meteorites and tend to look a lot like lava on Earth or on the Moon. Very few changes have taken place in the achondrites—almost no melting or chemical changes.

The chondrite group of meteorites is divided into two types: ordinary chondrites and *carbonaceous* (carbon-bearing) *chondrites.* The carbonaceous chondrites are a much smaller, rarer group. In many ways, they are the most exciting of all types of meteorites. They date back 4.5 billion years to the beginning of the solar system, and scientists believe that these meteorites have retained many of the characteristics

Notice the many round chondrules throughout this slab cut from an ordinary chondrite, ALH77278.

common to the earliest structures of that time. Carbonaceous chondrites have undergone very little heating because water remains within their structures, bound up inside minerals. Other volatile elements and compounds also remain. These strange, dark rocks have undergone far fewer changes than any other type of rock during the billions of years since the solar system first formed.

Jigsaw Meteorites

Every type of meteorite has several subtypes, and just to keep us hopping, many individual meteorites are made up of pieces of more than one type of space rock. Some meteorites are made up of different types of fragments glued together in an assortment called *breccia*. These sharply angled fragments probably came together sometime in the meteorite's history, when one body slammed into another of a different composition. A finely grained cementing mixture was formed that glued together the chunks of unrelated material. Scientists occasionally find chondrite, achondrite, and stony-iron materials cemented together in one space rock!

Searching in Frozen Antarctica

In 1969 a group of geophysicists from Japan found out that literally thousands of meteorites lie strewn on the ice fields or frozen just beneath the surface of Antarctica. Even though meteorites fall in all areas of our planet, Antarctica is ideal for finding them because the dark rocks show up clearly against the white background of the ice fields. The meteorites are well preserved, undisturbed by heavy sedimentation. Scientists reason that almost anything they find besides ice on the East Antarctic Ice Sheet most likely came from space. This is helpful because it is unlikely that ordinary-looking rocks there are, in fact, ordinary. In some areas, the concentration of meteorites is as high as one every few steps.

Within ten years, American and Japanese teams had found pieces of approximately three thousand meteorites. These have been stored in sterile conditions either in NASA's lunar rock curatorial facility or in Tokyo, Japan. Annual visits to Antarctica by NASA scientists and other research teams continue. Searchers scramble across the ice to gather the treasure, and cries of "Here's one" ring out as they fight the freezing Antarctic wind. Some of the most exciting samples ever found have come from these ice fields.

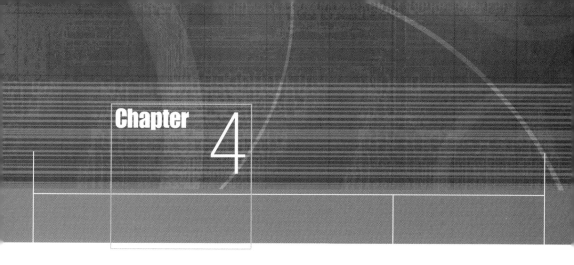

Chapter 4

Big Impacts and Earth's Scars

The telescope was a brand-new invention in the early 1600s that was designed for viewing faraway objects more clearly. When telescopes were first available, most people used them to spot ships at sea. However, the great Italian astronomer Galileo Galilei came up with a bright idea. He thought he would try turning his telescope toward objects in the nighttime sky. One night in 1609, he looked at the Moon with his new gadget. He discovered that the Moon's surface was pockmarked by thousands of round pits. Galileo gave a name to these pits—the Latin word *crater,* which means "mixing bowl."

Yet no one could be certain about what caused these craters. Were they carved out by explosive volcanoes? Did giant gas bubbles become trapped in the molten lava deep beneath the Moon's surface and then

Galileo Galilei.

rise to the surface and burst, leaving these big pits? Or did thousands of objects collide with the Moon with such explosive force that their impacts produced these scars? Over the centuries, astronomers discovered that every object in the solar system was covered with craters.

D.M. Barringer: The Man Who Wouldn't Quit

When Daniel Moreau Barringer began looking at a big crater in Arizona, most geologists assumed that the crater had been created by a volcano. They couldn't really explain how it was formed, though, and Barringer didn't think it was volcanic in origin at all. He thought something really big had hit Earth's surface—hard. And the huge, nearly 1-mile (1.6 km) -wide crater was the result.

Barringer consulted with a physicist named Benjamin C. Tilghman, who was also an expert in explosives. The two men examined the rocks and debris along the rim of the crater. They took soil samples from the crater floor. They found evidence that caused them to think that a large, nickel-iron meteorite had caused the crater.

So Barringer began mining. He found a deposit of fused quartz glass, a substance not produced by volcanoes. Since Barringer's time, scientists have learned that fused quartz glass may form when a large space rock hits Earth. It was the first strong piece of evidence that Barringer was probably right in his theory about the crater's formation.

Barringer fought for his point of view for twenty-seven years and lived to see confirmation that Meteor Crater was indeed caused by a meteorite impact. Unfortunately, he never did find the big deposit of nickel-iron that he was looking for. It had apparently vaporized during the impact explosion.

Objects with thick atmospheres, such as Earth and Venus, had fewer of them. Objects with no atmosphere, such as the Moon and the planet Mercury, had so many craters that they had scars on top of scars.

Dents in Earth

Scientists have discovered that a period of intense collisions known as the heavy bombardment occurred early in the history of the solar system. Earth was subjected to enormous impacts, as was every other planet, moon, and asteroid at that time. We also know that the rate of collision slowed down, but collisions continue to occur. Scientists have found craters on Earth that date back hundreds of millions of years and some that are only fifty thousand years old.

When a Space Rock Falls to Earth

Because an incoming meteor travels toward Earth at a speed of at least 6 miles (10 km) per second, a large meteorite can dig a hole of considerable size. When it slams into Earth's surface, its energy flings crushed rock and earth into the air. In the process, a cavity forms where it hit. The floor of the crater is covered with broken material (breccia). Fractures in the rock beneath the crater may extend downward and outward a distance of as much as three times the depth of the crater. Layers of rock, or *strata,* at the edges of the crater are jumbled. Around the edges of the crater, a high rim forms from the rock and soil that was thrown outward and upward by the impact (ejected material), along with the upturned strata. Ejected material also flies over the rim and settles in the surrounding area. This material is known as the *ejecta blanket* and covers the surrounding surface with dust, rock, and debris. Large chunks of ejected rock may also crash into Earth with such force that they form secondary craters of their own.

A bolide typically explodes when it impacts Earth. So, scientists have gained a lot of insight into how impact craters form by studying test explosions of TNT. At the base of the fireball, a dense, turbulent cloud forms from a mixture of soil and expanding gas. When the dust settles, dunelike *hummocks* form from the deposits. Powerful, high-speed jets angle outward—probably in much the same way that material is thrown outward by a meteorite impact.

Visiting Meteor Crater

If you have a chance to visit Meteor Crater, stand near the rim and look down into the vast cavity. Imagine a time when the land stretched smoothly across that area. Then imagine a huge rock barreling out of the sky and slamming with enormous force into Earth's surface. The jumbled strata at your feet are witnesses to that impact. Dirt, dust,

Barringer Crater (Meteor Crater) clearly marks the spot near Winslow, Arizona where a small meteorite hit about 50,000 years ago. The crater is about 3,960 feet (1,200 m) across.

rock, and fire shot upward and outward. A shock wave rumbled across what is now the Arizona desert. Animals and plants in the surrounding area were wiped out in moments. This huge, well-preserved crater is one of the best testimonies to a process that has occurred over and over in the solar system and on our planet. It is an overwhelming sight.

A Few Big Dents: Meteorite Impact Craters on Earth

Vital Statistics

Location	Approximate Age (in years)	Estimated Size of Crater
BARRINGER CRATER (METEOR CRATER), FLAGSTAFF, ARIZONA	50,000	3,960 feet (1,200 m)
ODESSA, TEXAS	50,000	528 feet (161 m)
CHICXULUB, MEXICO	65 million	62 miles (100 km)
MJØLNIR CRATER, BARENTS SEA	150 million	1.25 miles (2 km)
MANICOUAGAN, QUEBEC, CANADA	212 million	62 miles (100 km)
ACRAMAN, AUSTRALIA	570 million	100 miles (160 km)
BEAVERHEAD, MONTANA	600 million	37 miles (60 km)
SUDBURY, ONTARIO, CANADA	1.85 billion	125 miles (200 km)
VREDEFORT, SOUTH AFRICA	1.97 billion	87 miles (140 km)

The Great Disappearance of the Dinosaurs

In 1980 a physicist named Luis Alvarez and his geologist son, Walter, announced a stunning new theory. They had evidence that led them to think that the extinction of the dinosaurs 65 million years ago was caused by the impact of a large meteoroid (or small asteroid) about 0.6 miles (1 km) in diameter. Their idea was controversial, but studies undertaken since then have shown that they were probably right. No meteorite impact that large or cataclysmic has occured since human beings began walking on Earth.

Luis (left) and Walter Alvarez.

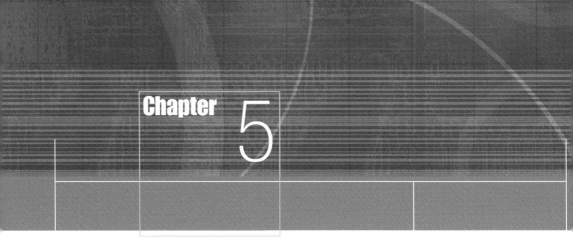

Chapter 5

Meteoroids: Source Material

When the solar system first formed, about 4.56 billion years ago, the Sun took shape from a huge cloud of dust and gas known as the *solar nebula*. As the Sun formed, leftover dust and gas began to clump into smaller, dense clouds traveling in orbit around the newborn star. As they traveled, they swept up more material out of the surrounding areas. The more material they gathered up, the bigger they got and the greater their gravitational pull. The particles of these large clumps coalesced, or united, to become the planets, including Earth. Smaller clumps of material were drawn into orbit around the planets, and became the moons, or satellites, of the planets.

Some small clumps of material were left over, though. These small clumps weren't big enough to attract a lot more gas and dust. They couldn't "sweep" material out of the surrounding area the way the planets did. So, one of five fates awaited them. Some got kicked out of the solar system like a home run hit in a baseball game—right out of the ballpark. Some collided with planets and broke up or became part of the planets. Some got captured into orbit around a planet. Some came close enough to the more massive planets that the small clumps were broken up into fragments by *tidal forces*. Finally, some are still out there, preserved intact, orbiting in space between the planets. These objects became comets, asteroids, and meteoroids.

So far, all the meteorites found on Earth have come from one of three sources: asteroids, the Moon, or Mars. Some other sources may

An artist's view of the solar nebula, from which the solar system was formed.

also exist. Material from comets generally disappears before reaching Earth, but some scientists think that fragments from Venus and possibly other planets could turn up on our doorstep. That hasn't happened—or at least no one has found any meteorites from other sources yet.

Asteroid Fragments

The vast majority of meteoroids are fragments of asteroids—the products of collisions, splintering, and fragmentation. Many of them have traveled for millions or even billions of years in their present forms.

In fact, for many years, *planetologists* assumed that asteroids were the only sources of meteorites. These scientists assumed that fragments that had been knocked off a planet or moon could not find their way to Earth's surface. However, after NASA astronauts brought tons of rocks back from the Moon and a pair of spacecraft called *Viking* visited Mars, scientists learned a lot more about those two bodies. They also learned what about these bodies could be considered unique. With this new information, they began looking at the question of whether meteorites could come from the Moon or Mars. The answer they came up with was this: Meteorites could come from either place, and a few already have.

Rocks from the Moon

It's not very hard to throw a rock off the Moon. The escape velocity (speed required for an object to escape the Moon's gravity) is only 1.48 miles (2.38 km) per second, which is not a lot faster than the speed required to send a bullet out of a rifle's muzzle.

It's a short hop from the Moon to Earth, so a lot of material hurled off the Moon by an impact lands on Earth soon afterward. However, some of the ejected rocks may enter an orbit around the Sun. Eventually, these may also eventually fall to Earth, but that can take millions of years.

You can distinguish a Moon rock, or lunar meteorite, from other meteorites by observing three main things.

This is the first color photo that was taken of the surface of Mars. This photo was taken by *Viking 1*.

First, it will have a mark of its voyage to Earth's surface from space—a fusion *crust* created by the melting that took place as the object plunged through Earth's atmosphere. Second, it will have a mark of its travels outside Earth's atmosphere—certain *isotopes* will be present that can be produced only by cosmic rays that never enter Earth's atmosphere. These isotopes could have formed only in outer space.

Lunar Meteorites

Vital Statistics

Name	Place Found	Year Found	Mass (grams)
(YAMATO-?) #1153	Antarctica	?	?
CALCALONG CREEK	Australia	~1990	19
YAMATO-791197	Antarctica	1979	52.4
YAMATO-793169	Antarctica	1979	6.1
YAMATO-793274	Antarctica	1980	8.7
ALLAN HILLS 81005	Antarctica	1982	31.4
YAMATO-82192/ 82193/86032	Antarctica	1982/1986	37 + 27 + 648 = 712
ELEPHANT MORAINE 87521/96008	Antarctica	1987/1996	31 + 53
ASUKA-881757	Antarctica	1988	442
MACALPINE HILLS 88104/88105	Antarctica	1989	61 + 663
QUEEN ALEXANDRA RANGE 93069/94269	Antarctica	1993	21.4 + 3.1

Third, it will have evidence of a lunar origin—*composition,* isotope ratios, minerals, and textures that match the Moon samples collected during the Apollo missions. For example, many rocks from the lunar highlands have a composition that is 75 to 80 percent plagioclase feldspar. This material appears to be relatively uncommon in asteroids, planets, and moons, so its presence helps indicate a lunar origin.

Name	Place Found	Year Found	Mass (grams)
QUEEN ALEXANDRA RANGE-94281	Antarctica	1994	23
DAR AL GANI 262	Libya, Africa	1997	513
DAR AL GANI 400	Libya, Africa	1998	1,425
YAMATO-981031	Antarctica	1998	186
DHOFAR 081/280 (PROBABLY PAIRED)	Oman	1999/2001	174 251
NORTHWEST AFRICA 032/479 (PROBABLY PAIRED)	Morocco	1999/2001	~300 + 156
DHOFAR 026	Oman	2000	148
DHOFAR 025	Oman	2000	751
NORTHWEST AFRICA 773 (3 STONES)	Western Sahara	2000	359 + 224 + 50 = 633
NORTHWEST AFRICA 482	probably Algeria	2000?	1,015
DHOFAR 287	Oman	2001	154

Visitors from Mars

About twenty-two thousand meteorites have been found on Earth's surface. Of those, only a handful—eighteen at last count in 2001—have been identified as having come from Mars. Martian meteorites are all achondrites and are known by the name SNC—the first initials of the three recognized types and the names of the localities where the first three examples were found: Shergotty, India (1865), Nakhla, Egypt (1911), and Chassigny, France (1815).

What makes scientists think that these meteorites came from Mars? First, their age. Most meteorites found on Earth are understood to have broken off from asteroids when they collided with each other, chiefly in the Main Asteroid Belt between Mars and Jupiter. Like the planets and the rest of the objects in the solar system, asteroids date back about 4.5 billion years, as they formed shortly after the Sun began to shine. Asteroids, though, are much smaller than the planets and most moons. Asteroids started out hot, like the rest of the solar system, but they soon cooled down. By now, they have been cold for a very long time. Therefore, most meteorites show signs of having been crystallized for the past 4.5 billion years.

SNC meteorites, though, seem to be much younger. They apparently solidified from molten rock only 1.3 billion to 200 million years ago. This is very recent, in terms of solar system time—and only planets are large enough to have stayed so hot for so long. The two nearest planets are Venus and Mars. However, Mars is a much more likely source of meteorites. The red planet is much smaller than Venus (which is about the size of Earth), so it has much less gravity and a much thinner atmosphere than Venus. As a result, rocks can collide with and escape from Mars more easily.

This illustration shows the Main Asteroid Belt between Mars and Jupiter. Jupiter is at the top right with its moon Io at the bottom right. At the top left is another of Jupiter's moons, Europa.

The most exciting evidence for a Martian origin came from tiny samples of gas that were found trapped within EETA79001, a meteorite found on the Elephant Moraine in Antarctica. The composition of this gas almost exactly matched the gases found by Viking experiments in 1976, when NASA sent lander spacecraft to test the Martian soils and atmosphere.

Mars also has volcanoes that have certainly been active within the last 1.3 billion years. Lava could have flowed from a volcano and cooled to form the *basalt* found, for example, in EETA79001. This could be the origin of recently cooled rock that made its way to our planet.

Mars also has impact craters on its surface, where large objects must have hit it. In the 1980s NASA scientists ran tests to see how fast an object would have to be moving to fling pieces of Mars into space. They found that if a large object struck Mars at 22,000 miles (35,000 km) per hour, the blow could knock chunks of rock off the surface at speeds well above the escape velocity

This meteorite was collected in 1979 from the Elephant Moraine region of Antarctica. Scientists believe this 15-pound (7-kg) rock is approximately 1.3 billion years old.

for Mars—11,185 miles (18,000 km) per hour. In fact, an impact could cause the sudden vaporization of permafrost below the Martian surface, and that could cause a massive explosion, which would send basalt rocks flying even more quickly into space.

Martian Meteorites
Vital Statistics

Name	Place Found	Year*	Classification	Mass (kg)
CHASSIGNY	Chassigny, France	1815	Chassignite	4 (approximate)
SHERGOTTY	Shergotty, India	1865	Shergottite	5 (approximate)
NAKHLA	Nakhla, Egypt	1911	Nakhlite	10 (approximate)
LAFAYETTE	Lafayette, Indiana	1931	Nakhlite	0.80 (approximate)
GOV. VALADARES	Governador Valadares, Brazil	1958	Nakhlite	0.16
ZAGAMI	Zagami, Nigeria	1962	Shergottite	18
ALH77005	Allan Hills, Antarctica	1978	Shergottite	0.48
EETA79001	Elephant Moraine, Antarctica	1980	Shergottite	7.90
ALH84001	Allan Hills, Antarctica	1984	none	1.90

Name	Place Found	Year	Classi-fication	Mass (kg)
LEW88516	Lewis Cliff, Antarctica	1988	Shergottite	0.013
Y19793605	Yamato Mountains, Antarctica	1993	Shergottite	0.018
QUE94201	Queen Alexandra Range, Antarctica	1994	Shergottite	0.012
DAR AL GANI 476** DAR AL GANI 489 DAR AL GANI 735 DAR AL GANI 670 DAR AL GANI 876	Sahara Desert, Libya	1998 1997 1996/1997 1998/1999 1998	Shergottite	2.015 2.146 0.588 1.619 0.006
LOS ANGELES 001** LOS ANGELES 002†	Los Angeles County, California	1999	Shergottite	0.453 0.245
SAYH AL UHAYMIR 005** SAYH AL UHAYMIR 008 SAYH AL UHAYMIR 051 SAYH AL UHAYMIR 094	Sayh al Uhavmir, Oman	1999 1999 2000 2001	Shergottite	1.344 8.579 0.436 0.223
DHOFAR 019	Dhofar, Oman	2000	Shergottite	1.056
NORTHWEST AFRICA 480	Algeria	2000	Shergottite	0.028
NORTHWEST AFRICA 817	Morocco	2000	Nakhlite	0.104

* Meteorites are listed in the order in which they were discovered.
** These meteorites from the same area are considered fragments of the same parent meteorite.
† Found in an amateur rock collection; date of fall or find unknown.

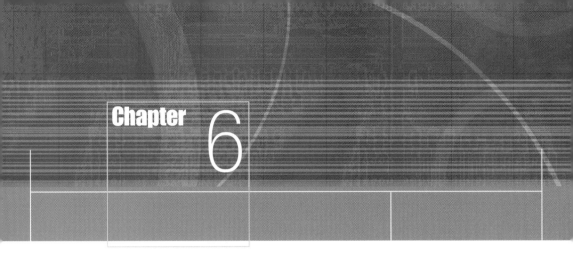

Chapter 6

Keeping
Watch

A lot has changed since 1803, when Jean-Baptiste Biot realized that the rocks he found at L'Aigle, France, came from space. Humanity has gained a new view of incoming meteoroids. Slowly, we have realized that meteoroids head our way over and over and have been hitting Earth's surface ever since the birth of the solar system. In the twentieth century, two discoveries contributed to this new view: the investigation that followed the Tunguska explosion in Siberia and the discovery of a 65-million-year-old crater on the Yucatan Peninsula in Mexico.

Taking a Look at Tunguska

Several years went by after the Tunguska explosion before investigators could reach the remote location. A few interviews were conducted with herdsmen in 1924, but no one actually visited the site until three years after the interviews. When researchers arrived in 1927, almost two decades after the event, they were stunned by what they *didn't* see. There was no impact crater. Apparently, the plummeting object had exploded in midair, just before reaching the ground. The devastation was still unsettling. Trees were felled in every direction, cutting a huge circle in the forest some 40 miles (60 km) in diameter. What was the object, though? Some researchers thought it must have been a comet. Others thought it was a meteoroid.

Computer simulations in the 1990s showed that a stony meteoroid could have caused the blast. It was probably about 150 to 200 feet (50 to 60 m) across—about one-half to two-thirds the size of a football field. In an effort to confirm the hypothesis, researchers returned once more to the site in 1994. At that point, they knew what they were looking for, and they found it—shards of a stony meteoroid embedded in the surrounding trees.

After the investigation of the Tunguska event, scientists began to realize that a tremendous asteroid impact could have a huge effect on living things. Also, after the invention of thermonuclear weapons in the 1940s and 1950s, scientists and leaders alike gained a new understanding of the consequences of a giant blast. They began to see that an enormous impact, like one that would occur during a nuclear war, would throw so much debris into the skies that the Sun's light would be blocked out for as long as a year or more. Plants in the surrounding territory would die, then animals would die, and finally nearly all life would be choked out.

Chicxulub and the Dinosaurs

One of the great mysteries of modern-day science has been the disappearance of the dinosaurs. For 165 million years, dinosaurs dominated Earth. They were the most populous and most successful creatures in existence. Today, few living descendants of the great dinosaurs exist. Birds and crocodiles are distant relatives, but the giant creatures that roamed Earth's surface in such great numbers are gone. They

This is an artist's illustration of an asteroid ending the reign of the dinosaurs.

disappeared from Earth about 65 million years ago. Scientists knew this from the geologic record, but no one knew exactly why they disappeared, until the Alvarezes suggested a giant meteoroid or asteroid impact. They based their hypothesis on the identification of an element called iridium in the geologic layer laid down at the time the last of the dinosaurs became extinct. Iridium is a substance that is extremely rare on Earth but is more common in objects in space. Researchers found that they could examine this layer of rock in many places around the world. It always showed unusually high amounts of iridium. Because this layer marks the transition between the Cretaceous period and the Tertiary period, it is called the K/T boundary layer (K for the German spelling of Cretaceous and T for Tertiary).

The Alvarez theory was very controversial at first. It seemed to be a big leap to make on the basis of just a high concentration of iridium in a rock layer. Since 1980, though, the evidence supporting the theory has grown remarkably. The traces of a huge crater were discovered beneath the land near a town called Chicxulub in Mexico and stretched beneath the waters of the Gulf of Mexico. In 1984 scientists also found bits of shocked quartz in the K/T boundary layer, as well as glassy spherules. These were more pieces of evidence that a giant impact with considerable force and heat had occurred.

All of the findings began to line up: A very large object probably smashed into Earth 65 million years ago in what is now eastern Mexico near the Caribbean Basin, where the K/T boundary layer is thickest and contains the largest glassy droplets. So the story of the dinosaurs' quick end becomes another lesson in the potential dangers posed by objects careening toward Earth from space.

Watching the Skies

Today a network of professional astronomers "watches" the skies nightly for new examples of near-Earth objects, including meteoroids, asteroids, and comets. These astronomers are especially concerned about those objects that cross Earth's orbit and are potentially hazardous to human life.

Nearby objects that don't currently cross Earth's orbit can also become dangerous. Their orbits can become *perturbed,* or altered by gravity, bringing the object into an Earth-crossing path.

Of course, scientists don't literally watch the skies with their eyes. They use high-tech telescopes, cameras, and computers equipped with CCDs (charge-coupled devices) to watch for them. This combination of equipment allows astronomers to perform automated searches of the skies for any objects that are unknown. The computer compares the view gathered by the telescope with all known databases of stars,

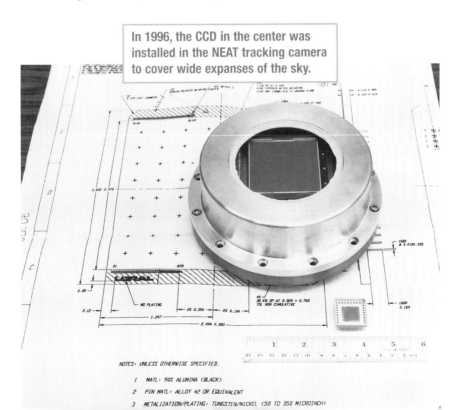

In 1996, the CCD in the center was installed in the NEAT tracking camera to cover wide expanses of the sky.

asteroids, comets, and Kuiper Belt objects. When the computer finds something that doesn't match the databases, it records the view. Researchers can review the results the next morning and decide whether anything looks suspicious. Then they plan the next night's search.

As of 2001, an international team of watchers had found nearly 1,400 close approaches, but no large objects on a collision course with Earth—aside from the usual meteor showers, fireballs, bolides, and small to medium-size meteorites.

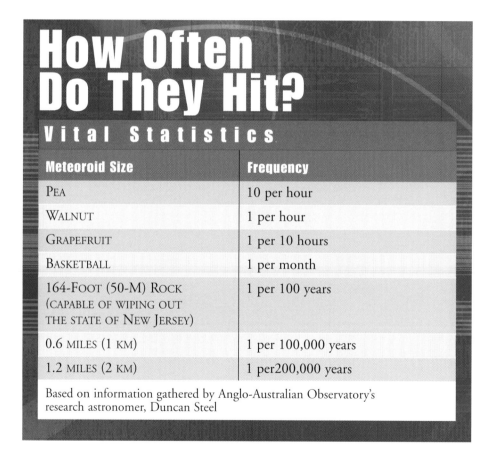

How Often Do They Hit?

Vital Statistics

Meteoroid Size	Frequency
PEA	10 per hour
WALNUT	1 per hour
GRAPEFRUIT	1 per 10 hours
BASKETBALL	1 per month
164-FOOT (50-M) ROCK (CAPABLE OF WIPING OUT THE STATE OF NEW JERSEY)	1 per 100 years
0.6 MILES (1 KM)	1 per 100,000 years
1.2 MILES (2 KM)	1 per200,000 years

Based on information gathered by Anglo-Australian Observatory's research astronomer, Duncan Steel

Chapter 7

Clues to the Universe

When you hold a meteorite in your hand, you know that you are holding a very old piece of the universe. This hard, dark, heavy object has lasted, with few changes to its structure, since almost the beginning of the solar system. For scientists, it holds clues to the unknown secrets of the universe. For these reasons, meteorites have a priceless value to humankind.

Meteorites: Seeds of Life?

Most scientists today think the evolution of life on Earth took place on Earth. Most past theories have centered on the development of life from chemicals that existed on our planet since its beginning.

The Murchison meteorite fell in Australia in 1969. These pieces are presently at the Melbourne Museum, in Museum Victoria.

However, some scientists think that Earth may have supplied only the environment—not the ingredients—for life. Earth's supply of organic materials may have come to Earth from elsewhere, carried to the surface in the constant "rain" of meteorites, comets, and dust that bombarded Earth in its early years. Researchers have discovered that a considerable variety of organic compounds can ride onboard all three of these kinds of objects. One meteorite class—carbonaceous chondrites—can have a composition that is as much as 5 percent organic material.

In September 1969, new evidence landed on Earth. A large fall of carbonaceous chondrite rock fell in Murchison, Victoria, Australia, near the city of Perth. Scientists found that material from the Murchison fall contained more than seventy different amino acids. Eight of these amino acids numbered among the approximately twenty basic ingredients for building proteins. Could the building blocks of life have ridden to Earth aboard a meteorite? The pieces of this carbonaceous chondrite looked like charcoal briquets strewn across a 5-mile (8-km) area. They had fallen in people's yards and in the streets. The townspeople gathered up hundreds of the small rocks, the largest of which weighed only 15 pounds (7 kg). The total weight amounted to about 220 pounds (100 kg). These meteorites were about 10 percent water, which made them very fragile. Luckily, they were gathered up quickly, or they might have been destroyed by the weather.

The Murchison fall was the second big fall of carbonaceous chondrites in 1969. The first took place in Pueblito de Allende, in the state of Chihuahua, Mexico. This huge fall dumped more than 2 tons of meteoritic material—more carbonaceous chondrite than had previously been found in the entire world.

Carbonaceous chondrites are especially interesting because of their high content of carbon and their high water contents. Most of the carbon is tied up in organic compounds, which naturally raises the possibility of a biological origin. Their presence in carbonaceous chondrites was first noticed in the nineteenth century, and each new meteorite find raises hopes that more clues will be found. Answers to two interesting questions could be tied up in the composition of these meteorites: How did life begin on Earth, and does life exist anywhere else in the universe?

The thinking goes like this: When planets first began forming in the disk of dust and gas around our Sun, the solar system was a violent place. Chunks of meteorites, asteroids, and *planetesimals* careened through space. They smashed into each other, knocked one another out of orbit, and whizzed on to collide with other objects. Cataclysmic explosions and collisions made the place into a cosmic war zone—so much so that scientists sometimes call this period the heavy bombardment.

Today, as meteorites continue to speed through the atmosphere and smack into Earth's surface, they may carry complex organic molecules (the building blocks required for life). These molecules are made up of the biogenic elements—that is, chemical elements that are used by living things. They include carbon, hydrogen, oxygen, nitrogen, phosphorous, and sulfur.

Through *radiocarbon dating* and other testing, scientists have discovered that many of the molecules they find inside meteorites today are as old as the solar system. These chunks of rock have been traveling around the solar system since they were first formed 4.5 billion years ago, and they have probably carried these molecules along from the beginning. So even though organic molecules may not have existed on Earth when our planet first formed, these molecules certainly arrived onboard the many meteorites that smashed into it in its first billion years. These "imported" organic molecules, some scientists believe, were the raw materials from which life eventually formed.

The Case of ALH84001

In 1996 another exciting discovery made headline news. The subject was a very plain-looking rock. It had been around since 1984, when it was found near the icy slopes of Allan Hills, Antarctica. However, it had been misclassified. Not until 1993 did scientists realize that ALH84001 was from Mars. When teams of scientists from NASA

Some scientists think Martian meteorite ALH84001 may hold clues to the origins of life.

began examining this small, black meteorite, they reported results that caused an enormous amount of excitement and controversy. The high level of interest engaged not just the scientific community but people from all walks of life throughout the world. NASA scientists, headed by David McKay, announced that they had found evidence of Martian life. They found not currently living organisms but what they believed to be fossils of very small organisms that lived on Mars approximately 3.6 billion years ago. The diameter of the largest of these structures is equal to 1/100th of the diameter of a human hair.

We know a little about the path taken by ALH84001 on its way from Mars to Earth. A meteorite slammed into Mars 16 million years ago and chipped off some fragments of surface rock. The fragments were hurled into space, where they traveled for millions of years. Finally, just eleven thousand years ago, one of these chips was pulled into Earth's gravitational field. It plunged through Earth's atmosphere and made a quick descent to the ice fields surrounding Allan Hills in Antarctica. Its Martian origin is virtually certain. Its mineral content is right and the gases sealed within the rock match the gases in the Martian atmosphere.

Here's what the NASA scientists found. First, there were very small structures that had irregular shapes that closely resembled microfossils found on Earth—remains of very primitive bacteria that lived on our planet 4 billion years ago. Unfortunately, most other scientists concluded that the "microfossils" from the meteorite were probably not organic structures at all, but simply inorganic mineral deposits. As the late exobiologist Carl Sagan once admonished, "Extraordinary claims require extraordinary evidence." In this case, the extraordinary claim was that evidence of Martian life had been discovered, and the evidence was certainly not extraordinarily strong. Many scientists conclude that inorganic explanations of the structures seem more likely than the explanation announcing the discovery of tiny fossils of ancient Martian life in ALH84001.

As of 2001 the case of ALH84001 was still not closed. The research team offered new information in 2000 and 2001: A mineral "chain of pearls" of a type that is only produced by living organisms on Earth had been found. The researchers found magnetite minerals of three types located inside the meteorite's carbonate globules. Two of the magnetite types could be produced through inorganic means. However, it was the third type that was intriguing. On Earth, the researchers explained, this group of magnetites could be produced only by living bacteria. Earthly bacteria use these chains of crystals to navigate by aligning the magnetic property of the magnetite with Earth's

This high-resolution scanning electron microscope image of meteorite ALH84001 shows an unusual tubelike structural form that is less than 1/100th of the width of a human hair. However, many scientists think these structures were probably formed by non-biological processes.

magnetic field. This type made up 25 to 30 percent of the magnetite in ALH84001's carbonate globules.

One problem that always haunts scientists studying meteorites is the possibility of contamination. What keeps terrestrial substances from becoming "part" of a meteorite? Perhaps the scientists are looking not at Martian structures at all, but at plain old Earth life. ALH84001 is no exception. The meteorites collected in Antarctica are handled with particular care from the time they are collected in the ice fields. Still, the meteorite has been on Earth for eleven thousand years. That is plenty of time for it to have picked up some bacteria. However, the researchers say they have ruled out contamination, and the structures they are pointing out in particular are enclosed inside carbonate globules within the meteorite. Other scientists claim that the structures could have come from Earth or could simply have been caused by weathering from thousands of years spent in the Antarctic ice fields. So the debate continues.

Yet the existence of life on Mars is not impossible. Hardy *extremophiles* on Earth can thrive in conditions just as harsh as the ones that exist on Mars. Just below the surface of the cold, dry rock of Antarctica's valleys thrives a layer of photosynthetic microorganisms. Surprisingly, unusually hardy bacteria left behind on the Moon by Apollo astronauts lived for two and a half years in the frigid vacuum of space. It is thought that life probably could have existed on Mars, at least in some primitive form. The big question is: Did it actually exist there?

Messengers from Space

Meteorites continue to furnish scientists with a wealth of information about the solar system. These chunks from beyond Earth's realm carry messages from the past, like bottles at sea containing news from faraway places. Scientists have gleaned a lot of information about the history of the solar system from these messengers.

Everyone can help in the scientific process. If you see a fireball, watch it carefully and note its direction and speed of travel. Note its altitude and location. Listen to the sounds it makes, if you can hear any. And report it right away. Your information could help experts find the fall, if there is one. If you're carrying a camera or video camera, record the event. If you find a meteorite, report it to the Smithsonian Institution or a nearby museum or university. You can be an important part of the scientific process.

Meteorites traveled great distances before coming to rest on the plains, deserts, streams, ocean floors, and mountainsides of Earth's surface. Many are pieces of the past. Some offer glimpses into the history of our Moon and Mars. A meteorite offers an exciting connection for all of us with the universe beyond.

The next time you see a meteorite, think about where it has been. Think about the meteoroid, planet, or moon it once was part of. Think about the arc it must have traced in the sky as it plunged through Earth's atmosphere, or the fireball that thundered across the sky. Consider the force with which it crashed into Earth's surface. This is an object with an exciting past—a piece of the solar system that is often so small that you can hold it in your hand.

Exploring Meteors: A Timeline

1805 — Jean-Baptiste Biot examines the fall at L'Aigle, France, and convinces the French Academy of Sciences that meteorites come from space.

1815 — A meteorite is discovered in Chassigny, France, that turns out to be a fragment from the planet Mars.

1833 — An enormous Leonid meteor shower is recorded, with more than 200,000 sightings per hour.

1866 — The Leonid meteor shower returns, as predicted from a study of past records.

1902 — Ellis Hughes stumbles across the huge Willamette meteorite and lays claim to it.

1905 — Daniel M. Barringer becomes the first to recognize an impact crater caused by a meteorite on Earth (now known as Barringer Crater or Meteor Crater in Arizona).

1908 — A meteoroid explodes over Tunguska in central Siberia.

1966 — After a long period of reduced activity, the Leonid meteor shower returns.

1969	The Allende meteorite falls in Mexico.
	The Murchison meteorite falls in Australia.
1980	Luis Alvarez and his son, Walter, announce their theory that the extinction of the dinosaurs was caused by the cataclysmic impact of a large meteorite.
1980s–90s	The Chicxulub impact crater is discovered.
1984	The meteorite ALH84001 is collected in Antarctica.
1993	ALH84001 is classified as a Martian meteorite.
1996	David McKay claims that he and his team have found evidence of ancient Martian life in the meteorite ALH84001.
2000	The American Museum of Natural History signs a historic agreement with the Confederated Tribes of the Grand Ronde Community of Oregon, respecting the spiritual importance of the Willamette meteorite for tribal worship while agreeing to continue displaying the meteorite as part of the museum's exhibit.

ablation—the process of heating and vaporization that removes material from a meteor speeding through Earth's atmosphere

achondrite—a stony meteorite that does not contain chondrules (See *chondrule*)

asteroid—a large—greater than 0.6-mile (1-km)—chunk of material not included in any planet during formation; part of a planet that has been broken off by a collision (See *meteoroid*)

atmosphere—gases surrounding a planet or moon

basalt—a dark-colored volcanic igneous rock

bolide—a fireball that explodes; another name for a fireball

breccia—a rock composed of angled fragments of other rocks glued together by a fine-grained cement

capstan—a machine used to move or raise heavy objects, consisting of a drum or post that can be rotated to wind a cable attached to the object to be moved

carbonaceous chondrites—a class of very old stony meteorites that contain chondrules as well as organic compounds (compounds including carbon and oxygen)

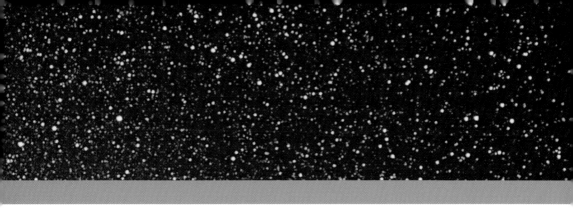

chondrite—a type of stony meteorite that contains chondrules (See *chondrule*)

chondrule—a small, spherical igneous rock that melted by some unknown process and recrystallized while floating in space. Chondrules are embedded in most chondrite meteorites.

comet—a small solar system object thought to originate far beyond the orbit of the planet Pluto and having a highly elongated orbit around the Sun; when traveling near the Sun it appears as a bright object, often having a long, bright tail.

composition—what something, such as a meteoroid or asteroid, is made of

constellation—a grouping of bright, visible stars in the nighttime skies, often imagined by ancient astronomers as outlines of familiar shapes, such as a lion (Leo), a warrior (Orion), or a queen (Cassiopeia)

core—the distinct region that is located at the center of a planet or moon. A body that has the same composition throughout is not said to have a core.

crater—a rimmed basin or depression in the surface of a planet or moon, caused by the impact of a meteoroid

crust—the outer surface of an object, such as a meteoroid, asteroid, planet, or moon

density—how much of a substance exists in a given volume

diameter—the distance across the center of a circle or sphere

ejecta blanket—a layer (blanket) of material tossed upward and outward by a meteorite hitting the surface of a planet or moon

elliptical—oval-shaped. Most orbits are elliptical.

erosion—the wearing away of a surface, such as by wind, water, or glacial ice

extremophile—an organism that thrives under extreme conditions that would kill most living things

fall—a meteorite that was observed as it fell through the atmosphere to Earth's surface

find—a meteorite that someone has found lying on or buried in the ground

fireball—an intensely bright meteor

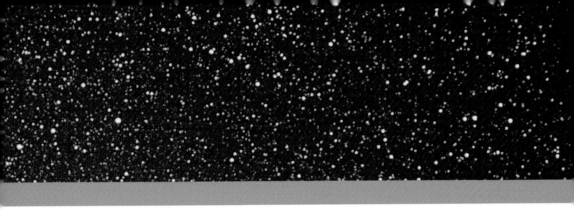

friction—the force that tends to slow or stop two bodies or substances sliding past each other when they are in contact. Friction causes energy to be given off in the form of heat.

gravity—the force that attracts two objects toward each other (for example, gravity attracts a person to Earth, a moon to a planet, or a planet to the Sun). The force of gravity depends on the masses of the two objects (a greater mass exerts a stronger pull) and how far they are from each other (the closer they are, the stronger the pull).

highly eccentric—describes an elliptical orbit that is much longer than it is wide

hummock—a low mound, small hill, or ridge

igneous rock—a rock that forms from the solidification of a liquid, often from melting followed by solidifying

inclusion—something that is included, such as an element embedded in a meteorite

ion—an atom that has an electrical charge because it has gained or lost one or more electrons

iron sulfide—a compound of iron and sulfur

isotopes—atoms of the same element that have slightly different masses because they have different numbers of a particle called a neutron. For example, the usual mass of carbon is represented by the number of protons and neutrons in its nucleus (12); carbon-14 is an isotope having 2 more neutrons, so it has 14 protons and neutrons.

kinetic energy—the energy of a body in motion

Kuiper Belt—the region of the solar system located just beyond Pluto's orbit and containing a variety of small, icy objects. It is named after Dutch-American astronomer Gerard P. Kuiper (1905–1973).

light-year—the distance light travels in a vacuum in one year, equal to 5.88 trillion miles (9.46 trillion km)

magma—molten rock material

magnetosphere—a vast region extending out from a planet. It is filled with electromagnetic radiation and electrically charged particles and is caused by the interaction of the planet's magnetic field and the solar wind.

Main Asteroid Belt—the region of the solar system where most asteroids are found, between the orbits of Mars and Jupiter

mantle—a geologically distinct region located below the crust of a planet and above its core

mass—the amount of material a body contains

meteor—a bright streak of light high in the sky caused by passage of a space rock through Earth's atmosphere

meteor shower—meteors that fall in a group, creating a spectacle resembling a rain shower of hundreds to thousands of lights in the sky, whose trails appear to originate from a single point in space

meteorite—a chunk of a rock from space that has struck the surface of a planet or moon

meteoriticist—a scientist who specializes in the study of meteors, meteoroids, and meteorites

meteoroid—a small—up to 0.6-mile (1-km)—chunk of material not included in any planet during formation; part of a planet that has been broken off by a collision (See *asteroid*)

olivine—a usually greenish mineral silicate composed of magnesium and iron that is common in some meteorites

Oort cloud—a region of the solar system, far beyond the orbit of Pluto, where comets are thought to originate. It is named after Dutch astronomer Jan Hendrix Oort (1900–1992).

orbit—the path traced by an object as it revolves around another body

ore—a rock or mineral containing something of value, usually a metal

perturb—to cause a variation in the orbit of a meteoroid or other object; usually caused by another object's influence

planetesimals—numerous small bodies thought to have orbited the Sun early in the development of the solar system, later gathering together to form planets

planetologist—a scientist who specializes in the study of solar system objects, especially planets and their moons

primordial—existing in the beginning or from the beginning (for example, of the solar system)

radiant point—a point in the sky from which meteors in a meteor shower seem to be falling; an illusion of perspective

radiocarbon dating—a method for determining the age of an object, such as a meteorite, by measuring the amount of carbon-14 it contains relative to other isotopes of carbon

radiometric dating—the process of determining the age of an object by measuring the relative amounts of certain isotopes (see *isotope*) within the object. Some isotopes are radioactive, and over time they decay to form different isotopes. The rate that a particular isotope (the parent) decays to form another isotope (the daughter) is constant. If you know how fast an isotope decays, then you can determine the age of an object by measuring the relative amounts of parent and daughter atoms. Carbon-14, for example, decays to nitrogen-14.

revolve—to move in a path, or orbit, around another object. The Earth revolves around the Sun, making a complete trip, or revolution, in one year.

rotate—to turn on an axis

siderophile elements—a group of elements that are attracted to metals. Examples include germanium, gallium, osmium, and iridium.

solar nebula—a primitive cloud of gas and material from which the Sun and the planets were born

solar wind—a stream of highly magnetic particles that flows at high speeds from the Sun's surface

spherule—a tiny ball or miniature sphere

sporadic meteor—a single meteor that is not part of a meteor shower

strata (pl. of stratum)—layers (for example, of rock)

tidal force—the difference in the force of gravity exerted on the near and far sides of an object

To Find Out More

The news from space changes fast, so it's always a good idea to check the copyright date on books, CD-ROMs, and videotapes to make sure that you are getting up-to-date information. One good place to look for current information from NASA is U.S. government depository libraries. There are several in each state.

Books

Campbell, Ann Jeanette. *The New York Public Library Amazing Space: A Book of Answers for Kids.* New York: John Wiley & Sons, 1997.

Dickinson, Terence. *Other Worlds: A Beginner's Guide to Planets and Moons.* Willowdale, Ontario: Firefly Books, 1995.

Gustafson, John. *Planets, Moons and Meteors.* New York: Julian Messner, 1992.

Spangenburg, Ray, and Kit Moser. *If an Asteroid Hit Earth.* New York: Franklin Watts, 2000.

Vogt, Gregory L. *The Solar System: Facts and Exploration.* Scientific American Sourcebooks. New York: Twenty-First Century Books, 1995.

CD-ROM

Beyond Planet Earth
Discovery Channel School
P.O. Box 970
Oxon Hill, MD 20750-0970
For the Macintosh and PC (DOS, Windows, OS2), from Discovery Channel School Multimedia, this is an interactive journey to the planets. It includes video from NASA and Voyager missions as well as more than two hundred photographs.

Video

Discover Magazine: Solar System
Discovery Channel School
P.O. Box 970
Oxon Hill, MD 20750-0970

Organizations and Online Sites

Many of the Web sites listed below are NASA sites, with links to many other interesting sources of information about meteoroids, meteors, meteorites, and the other objects of the solar system. You can also sign up to receive NASA news on many subjects via e-mail.

The Antarctic Search for Meteorites (ANSMET)

http://www.cwru.edu/affil/ansmet/index.html

This site answers frequently asked questions and provides background and information about the search for meteorites in Antarctica.

Asteroid and Comet Collisions

http://www.spaceref.com/Directory/Astronomy/Asteroids_And_Comets

This site provides a page of links to organizations that maintain a sky watch for Earth-crossing asteroids and comets.

The Astronomical Society of the Pacific

http://www.astrosociety.org

390 Ashton Avenue

San Francisco, CA 94112

The Astronomy Café

http://www2.ari.net/home/odenwald/cafe.html

This site answers questions and offers news and articles relating to astronomy and space by astronomer and NASA scientist Sten Odenwald.

Mars Meteorites (JPL)

http://www.jpl.nasa.gov/snc

NASA's Jet Propulsion Laboratory (JPL) tracks the latest news on meteorites from Mars.

Meteorite and Impacts Advisory Committee to the Canadian Space Agency

http://wwwdsa.uqac.uquebec.ca/~mhiggins/MIAC/MIAC.html

This site provides information about Canadian finds, falls, craters, and cratering, including photos, drawings, and information about types of meteorites.

Meteorites from Mars (JSC)

http://www-curator.jsc.nasa.gov/curator/antmet/marsmets/contents.htm

NASA's Johnson Space Center (JSC) presents a well-organized Internet site that provides an excellent overview of meteorites from Mars.

NASA Ask a Space Scientist

http://image.gsfc.nasa.gov/poetry/ask/askmag.html#list

This is an interactive page where NASA scientists answer your questions about astronomy, space, and space missions. It also offers archives and fact sheets.

NASA Newsroom

http://www.nasa.gov/newsinfo/newsroom.html

This site provides NASA's latest press releases, status reports, and fact sheets. It includes the NASA news archives for past reports and a search button for the NASA Web. It also allows you to sign up for e-mail versions of all NASA press releases.

The Nine Planets: A Multimedia Tour of the Solar System
http://www.seds.org/nineplanets/nineplanets/nineplanets.html
This site includes excellent material on Saturn and other planets from the Students for the Exploration and Development of Space at the University of Arizona.

The Planetary Society
http://www.planetary.org
65 North Catalina Avenue
Pasadena, CA 91106-2301
The Planetary Society is a nonprofit, nongovernmental organization that encourages the search for extraterrestrial life and planetary exploration. This site provides current planetary news and a learning center where you can view art, read journals, and find fun activities.

Rose Center for Earth and Space (Hayden Planetarium)
http://www.amnh.org/rose/index.html
This site includes a feature on the Willamette meteorite.

Sky Online
http://www.skypub.com
This is the site for *Sky and Telescope* magazine and other publications of Sky Publishing Corporation. This site has a good weekly news section on general space and astronomy news. It also contains many good tips for amateur astronomers, as well as a nice selection of links. A list of science museums, planetariums, and astronomy clubs organized by state can help you locate nearby places to visit as well.

Windows to the Universe

http://www.windows.ucar.edu

This NASA site, developed by the University of Michigan, includes sections on "Our Planet," "Our Solar System," "Space Missions," and "Kids' Space." You can choose from presentation levels of beginner, intermediate, and advanced. To begin exploring, go to the URL above and choose "Enter the Site."

Places to Visit

Check the Internet (*www.skypub.com* is a good place to start), your local visitor's center, or your local phone directory for planetariums and science museums near you. Here are a few other suggestions.

Ames Research Center

Moffett Field, CA 94035

http://www.arc.nasa.gov

Located near Mountain View and Sunnyvale on the San Francisco Peninsula, Ames Research Center welcomes visitors. This NASA branch heads the search for extraterrestrial life. Drop-in visitors are welcome and admission is free.

Exploratorium
3601 Lyon Street
San Francisco, CA 94123
http://www.exploratorium.edu
This museum offers internationally acclaimed, interactive science exhibits, including exhibits on astronomy subjects.

Jet Propulsion Laboratory (JPL)
4800 Oak Grove Drive
Pasadena, CA 91109
http://www.jpl.nasa.gov/pso/pt.html/
Tours are available of this facility once or twice a week by arrangement. See the site for instructions, or telephone or write to the JPL visitor contact. JPL is the primary mission control center for most NASA planetary missions, including the Pioneer, Voyager, and Cassini-Huygens missions to Saturn and its neighborhood.

National Air and Space Museum
7th and Independence Avenue, S.W.
Washington, DC 20560
http://www.nasm.si.edu/nasm/visit/visit.html/
This museum is located on the National Mall, west of the Capitol building.

Index

Bold numbers indicate illustrations.

Ray Spangenburg and **Kit Moser** are a husband-and-wife writing team specializing in science and technology. They have written forty-six books and more than one hundred articles, including a five-book series on the history of science and a four-book series on the history of space exploration. As journalists, they covered NASA and related science activities for many years. They have flown on NASA's Kuiper Airborne Observatory, covered stories at the Deep Space Network in the Mojave Desert, and experienced zero gravity on experimental NASA flights out of NASA Ames Research Center. They live in Carmichael, California, with their Boston terrier, F. Scott Fitz.